SUCCESS:FULL LIVING

HOW TO MAKE LIFE'S BUILT-IN
SUCCESS MECHANISM WORK FOR YOU

BY JUSTIN BELITZ, *O.F.M.*

Knowledge Systems, Inc.
INDIANAPOLIS, INDIANA

Published by Knowledge Systems, Inc.

For a free catalog or ordering information
call (317) 241-0749 or write Knowledge Systems,
7777 West Morris Street, Indianapolis, IN 46231 USA

Printed on acid-free, recycled stock.
First printing: May, 1991

About the artwork: Eileen Cantlin Verbus works as a creative illustrator, designer, painter and sculptor. Her unconstrained creative energy and depth of spirit perception shine through each illustration. Both author and publisher are deeply grateful for her gifts and are privileged by the opportunity to share them through this medium. She may be contacted at: P.O. Box 332, Hinckley, OH 44233.

Library of Congress Cataloging-in-Publication Data
Belitz, Justin.
    Success : full living : how to make life's built-in success
  mechanism work for you / by Justin Belitz
        p.   cm.
    Includes bibliographical references.
    ISBN 0-941705-17-X : $14.95
    1. Success--Religious aspects--Christianity. I. Title
  BV4598.3.B44 1991
  158'.1--dc20   91-13141
                                    CIP

10 9 8 7 6 5 4 3 2 1

DEDICATION

With tender love
        and gratitude
        I dedicate this book

To Daddy, Ma,
        sister Maryś,
        Joanie, brother Jack

Charlotte, Jimmy,
        Phyllis, Joey
        all who taught me life.

May God bless you!
        Just your being
        helps me stay on track.

CONTENTS

FOREWORD

It is very difficult to live in the world we live in without being immobilized by fear. Many of us fall in the trap of feeling that we are victims of the world or circumstances in it. If something is going wrong with our life, there is a great temptation to immediately find someone to blame. There is often a reluctance to want to take responsibility for whatever happens to us and to realize that it is only our own thoughts that can hurt us.

There are many who have found outer success but have found very little inner success. It may be very difficult to find a sense of inner peace living in a world which continues to see value in anger, hate and wars.

We all need as much help as we can get. *Success:Full Living* offers us a wonderful road map to inner peace and to a balance of inner and outer success. It is written simply and with clarity. It shows us the way to see light in a world that so often seems to be filled with darkness. It creates a tapestry for our finding a balance and simplicity in our lives. Above all, it emphasizes the importance of letting God and unconditional love come first in our lives.

I happen to favor books that are practical and not too abstract and this book is very clear about its practical applications. The chapter on Attitudes is most helpful. Most important, it stresses that joy and happiness are what life can really be all about. It is "happy reading" that can lead to one's own spiritual transformation. The choice for living a life filled with inspiration, creativity, and of helping others is always ours. May your journey be a more blessed one filled with love, joy and peace after reading this book.

—*Gerald G. Jampolsky, M.D.*
Tiburon, California

INTRODUCTION TO YOUR SUCCESS MECHANISM

I believe that all people are on this planet for the purpose of enjoying life. In the Old Testament God led the chosen people to a "land flowing with milk and honey." In the New Testament Jesus said, "I came that you may have life and have it to the full." In the Far East, the Buddha represents the human who found perfect peace. Because I believe that all major religions seek to lead human beings to an understanding of life, I also believe that we are here to enjoy friends, family, health, happiness, all the material things that we need, love, joy, peace, as well as all that is good, true and beautiful.

But you and I know there are people on the planet who are not experiencing fullness. What then is the problem?

From a theological perspective, when fullness is not achieved, there is nothing wrong with God. God dwells within each human being, but we all have free will. If we allow God to work through us then we can expect to experience fullness, but if we do not pay attention to the inner direction that comes from God and do "our own thing," we can expect to experience limit. *We* create limit in our lives.

From a human perspective, life is the result of the choices we make. As I travel across the globe sharing with people of every nation, race, religion, age, cultural and economic background, I see people coming to understand the simple ideas presented in this book, putting them into practice, and experiencing the fullness described above.

A teenager, for example, wanted to excel in cross-country running. When we first met, he was on a cross-country team at Padua High School where I was teaching. For three consecutive years, he had consistently been the worst cross-country runner on the team. When he heard the explanation of the Life Mechanism and how it could be applied to athletic ability, he immediately went to work setting specific goals and taking the time to visualize those goals daily in his mind. At the end of the season he was not only the best cross-country runner on the team, but he won the district competition and was invited to state.

In Houston a young couple was having problems in their relationship as well as with their children. They directed their Life Mechanism toward the achievement of personal growth and then to family relationships. In a matter of one week they were able to turn their lives in a completely different direction and today are not only prosperous in business but have established a successful pattern of family life for themselves and their children.

I have also seen older people who have taken the time to learn about the Life Mechanism and applied it to health. Many of these people were able to overcome illness, even terminal illness, and get a whole new lease on life.

The purpose of this volume is to help you understand your Life Mechanism as it works within you. It is a simple process that can be understood by anyone. All you need for success is an understanding of the process and the desire to make it work.

Not too long ago after a television presentation in Indianapolis, a gentleman from the audience approached me with the comment, "Justin, your presentation is very interesting but it sounds so simple." My response was, "It is!" I don't believe that God would demand that everyone have a Ph.D. before they can be successful in life. If the process is to be available to everyone, it must be simple.

My grandmother came to the United States from Poland with no education and with only the few things that she could carry in a single suitcase. She never learned the English language well, but she was very sensitive to the life process. As a result, she was successful with her family, her business, her community and, above all, her heart. She took what she knew and put it into practice. I think, perhaps, she was one of the greatest teachers of the Life Mechanism for me.

Your life is your responsibility. Will you allow it to just "happen"? Or, will you choose to "live it up!"?

1

THE LIFE MECHANISM

The Process

I suppose there are as many ways to describe the life process as there are people who are living it. What follows is a compilation of study and experience I have gathered over the years. This material has worked for me; hopefully it will help your life journey.

These ideas are certainly not new, although the manner in which they are presented may be unique. I would hope that you will take from this presentation whatever you can use and simply leave the rest.

Life

It has been my experience that the majority of people misunderstand the full meaning of the term "life." They believe that life is the process of putting all the pieces together so that eventually they can arrive at the place where they will "live happily ever after." This may sound unrealistic, but consider the numbers of people who are looking for the place called "security," "success," or "retirement."

The fact of the matter is: **Life is not a place of arrival; it is a manner of traveling.** Life by its very nature means "change" and only those who are comfortable with change will understand and enjoy life.

Unfortunately, many young people, unhappy with their present life situation, are looking for a better "place" in the future. When I was teaching high school students I frequently heard this kind of comment, "You know, Father, this high school experience is for the birds but when I get out of here and get a job, then my life will be happy." After a few years I would see the same individuals—now complaining about their work, having a difficult time dealing with fellow employees, finding the pay insufficient and generally unhappy. At that point they were saying, "When I find my life's partner, then I'll be successful." After a few years of experience, however, they find that marriage demands a great deal of work and is not always a pleasant experience. By that time they are saying, "When our first child comes...." As parents they find themselves up all night, working all day, and saying, "This can't be it!" So they continue to look into the future for the day "when the house will be paid for." When that happens, however, and there are a few more children, they are looking forward to the day "when the kids leave the house...." On and on it goes until finally they anticipate retirement.

The problem with this scenario is that the people involved are always looking into the future for a place of arrival where everything will be perfect. The reality is: no such place exists. They are never going to reach a place where they will "live happily ever after."

As we said above, life is motion; and if we want to be truly alive we have to go with the flow.

Life can be compared to a mountain stream. As long as the water is moving and flowing it's beautiful. So it is with life. As long as it's moving and flowing, life can be healthy and productive. However, if you take the same water and put it into a bucket, it will soon become stagnant; leave it there long enough and it will become putrid. Life is like that too. If you allow yourself to get into a rut or an unchanging routine, your life will become dull. Stay there long enough and you will put into place all of the circumstances that can bring on illness and even death.

It has always amazed me that we tend to understand this process in one area of life but are unable to apply it in other areas of life. Parents, for example, who bring a newly born infant into their home are thrilled to watch the child growing, learning, and changing daily in many different ways. If they do not see change over the period of a week they take the baby to a doctor. They know that growth and change are signs of healthy life. On the other hand, these same parents may create a schedule and then get very upset when they cannot keep to it, or when someone or something forces them to change it. If they could only shift their thought process to, "My schedule is only a guide from which to deviate," they could make necessary adjustments during the day and simply enjoy the experience.

In reality all of us are different today than we were yesterday. Tomorrow we will be different still—hopefully better. We are changing!

Success

When dealing with life, we all want to think in terms of success. Deep down inside each of us, there is a desire to "make it happen" so that somehow daily experience makes sense.

However, most people misunderstand the term "success." The dictionary, which is a statement of the consensus of the population, describes success as an "accomplishment" or "favorable termination of an event." People who begin a business, for example, may work for years before they achieve financial stability. Only at that point do they consider themselves to be successful. This definition describes success as a place of arrival, a concept that does not fit with the idea of life as "change" or "motion."

If you want to be consistent, you will have to change the definition of success. It is true that you must have a goal in life—you have to know where you are going. At the same time it is necessary to know where you are right now. If you clarify these two points and make a decision to move from one to the other, you will have a sense of purpose and your life will take on meaning; you will experience success. You can define success, therefore, as "being on the way to a clearly defined goal." This definition implies movement and, therefore, fits with the concept of life as we have described it.

A good example lies within the story of any young couple preparing for marriage. They can tell you exactly when they were engaged and when the marriage will take place. Sometimes the journey from the engagement to the wedding can take months, but long before the wedding day arrives they can tell you how the details will happen. They will know what they are going to wear, who will be in the wedding party and what they will wear, what kind of flowers will be carried, who will officiate at the ceremony, who will attend, what the music will be, where and when the reception will take place, what the menu will be and on and on. During this time of preparation these are exciting people to be with, because they are fulfilling the definition of success. They are on their way to a clearly defined goal.

Frequently, however, when the couple returns from their honeymoon they apply the first definition of success. They set up a household and breathe a sigh of relief, thinking, "Now we are successfully married." If they get stuck in this place they call "success," their lives get boring. They get up in the morning, go to work, come home, eat, watch television and go to sleep. The next day they get up in the morning, go to work, come home, eat, watch television and go to sleep, etc., etc., etc. If they do not have any further direction, their lives get very dull.

Where there is no excitement in the relationship, frequently each person will start looking outside the relationship for a more interesting life experience. Both then experience a great deal of stress. Often, as a counselor, I have helped couples in similar circumstances by suggesting a simple technique. I ask them to put on a sheet of paper a date at least five years into the future. Over the period of a week each is to separately describe how they want that day to go. In great detail they are to describe what the bedroom looks like, what kind of clothes they put on, what kind of breakfast they have and whether they serve themselves or are served. They picture what the house looks like, other people in the house, what time they leave, what kind of car they drive, what the neighborhood looks like, the city they are in, where they go to work, and what that reflects financially. They image where and with whom they have lunch, what kind of recreation they take and with whom, their evening meal, etc., etc. They are not allowed to work on the project together or to share ideas. After a week, they come back and explain their dreams in detail to me and to each other. I gather from their descriptions anything that may be the same or similar and help them to describe what could be their future marriage. When the couple takes the time to work through this exercise for a period of weeks, clearly identifying where they want their relationship to go and agreeing on their goals, each will automatically start moving toward the same ideal and, as they get closer to the goal, they get closer to each other and fall in love again.

This solution may sound simple. It is. The tragedy, as I see it, is that in our society too many of us spend more time planning our vacations than we do planning our lives.

Retreat centers around the world exist specifically for this latter purpose. They offer programs that help participants separate from everyone and everything and, in quiet, determine what it is that they want to do with their future lives. Once they have clear direction, they can begin moving in that direction and experience success. They will then be "on their way" to a clearly defined goal. This book can help you to do just that!

Action

Since movement from one point to another is essential to our definition of life success, the only measuring stick for success is effectiveness of action. In education, teachers cannot judge the success of the students by what they *say* but only by what they can *do*. If teachers want to know what their students understand about math, for example, all they have to do is present a problem and watch the students perform. They can then understand exactly what the students know and what they do not know.

In business this same norm applies. Job descriptions indicate what employees are to do, and supervision is nothing more than watching the performance of the employees.

This method of judging success is much more ancient than our educational system. In the Old Testament, Abraham was told by God to build a nation. Because he got busy doing God's plan, he was able to experience success.

Even in the New Testament Jesus said, "I came to do the will of my heavenly Father." He knew what the goal was and spent his life moving toward and achieving that goal.

Recently I went to a local office where I had an appointment with a young woman who was helping me on a project. I walked into the office to find the receptionist busy at a computer. As soon as I entered, she stopped her work, greeted me with a smile and asked: "How can I help you?" I asked for Sheryl and she immediately got on the phone. After successfully making contact, she invited me to be seated for a few seconds. She immediately went back to her work at the computer. When the phone rang, she gave her full attention to the person at the other end, quickly connecting her with her party. She then went back to the work at the computer while I was thinking: "She is a wonderful receptionist!"

On the other hand, I had occasion to walk into an office where the receptionist was engaged on the phone in an obviously personal conversation with a friend. I had to wait a long time before I was even acknowledged. After some time, holding her hand over the receiver, she curtly asked me: "What do you want?" When I mentioned the party I intended to see, she responded: "I'll be with you in a minute." She went back to her conversation and after a few minutes she put her caller on hold and made the contact for me. Without inviting me to take a seat, she said: "He's busy but he'll be out in a few minutes." Back again she went to her conversation while her typewriter sat quietly by and waited also.

The way we act clearly indicates in what areas we are successful. Actions do indeed speak louder than words!!!

Oftentimes, however, many of us find ourselves acting in one way when we really would prefer to be acting in another way. The question now arises: "How do we control our actions?" "How can I get myself to move in the direction I want to go?"

The answer to this question leads us to the topic of motivation.

Motivation

Have you ever been in a situation where you knew exactly what you were to do but you just couldn't get yourself to do it? On the other hand, recall a time when you looked forward to doing something—you not only anticipated the activity but when you got involved it was with a great deal of enthusiasm.

In each of these cases there is either a power to get you to move or a lack of that energy. It is this mysterious power that is referred to as motivation. I say "mysterious" because it is a concept that is used universally but few seem to know what it means!

Suppose a set of parents are dealing with a teenage child who is not interested in going to classes or doing homework. Trying to help, they tell the youngster, "You have got to get motivated!" The fact of the matter is that the child is very motivated but not in the direction of school. He or she is eager to be with friends, to attend athletic activities, dances and parties. The problem is the student isn't motivated toward study.

The same is true of a salesperson who is not producing results and who is called in by a sales manager, "You've got to get yourself motivated!" But that statement is not really understood by the sales person. The interior response may be, "I just don't like trying to push people into buying something they may not want or need," or "I am afraid the people I talk to will say 'No!' and I will feel stupid." On the other hand, this same person enjoys being with other colleagues and spends a lot of time with them.

The question here is: How can one activate the power of "motivation" in the direction they really want to go?

Let me use an illustration from my own life. When I first began to teach high school, I wanted to be effective—I wanted to help the students achieve so they could improve the quality of their lives.

After several years of teaching, however, I got into a rut—teaching the same subject day after day and using the same book and outline every year. At one point, I was so bored I did everything to distract myself. I got away as soon as I could at the end of each day, did only what was essential, talked about all the problems and sometimes dreaded going into the classroom.

In an effort to put some meaning into my life and to find some enjoyment in my work, I decided to go back to school to get an M.A. in my field—General Music Education. It was during this time I realized I didn't really know what the purpose of my class was supposed to be. I was just following a text and expecting the students to do the same. Eventually, I came to understand that if *I* didn't know the purpose of the class, how could the students know? If they didn't understand the purpose, why would they want to get involved?

Slowly, over two years and with the help of my professors, I was able to clarify the goal of the course. In fact, I was able to put it into a single statement: The purpose of my class is to teach my students to hear melody, rhythm, harmony, tone color, texture and form in any piece of music.

Once the goal became clear, it was possible to examine the content of the course and find what was appropriate and what was not. I began to remove irrelevant material and collect new. Soon I realized the present text simply would not do the job, and I began a search for another. It didn't take long to discover that the perfect text didn't exist—it had to be created. This was a project that took five years to complete.

During those five years my interest grew in a new approach to teaching. I found myself actively involved again in classroom activities, looking forward to class each day and seeking solutions to problems rather than concentrating on the problems themselves. My life was exciting again and I was motivated daily.

What I learned in this important life experience was: **Motivation is controlled by two very tangible and measurable commodities—goals and attitudes.**

Goals

Each day, we human beings are busy achieving some kind of objective. In some places in the world people awaken each morning and determine simple and basic goals like where to find food for the day, how to be protected from the elements of nature, etc.

In our own lives, we have to provide the same needs, but we add to the list. "I have to get to work so that I can make money to provide for living space and food." "I think I will go to a movie this evening." "I want to plan for a trip to Acapulco." "I want to learn more about the world and myself."

No matter who you are or where you live you do indeed have goals to achieve each day. It is these goals that put meaning into your life. A college student who has a passion to become a doctor has that goal in the back of their mind every day. Going to class and spending long hours in study makes sense only because it is related to a goal that is sometimes many years ahead. Parents go to work each day because they want the means to provide a good education for their children and to provide those things they determine to be important for life. Even elderly people, totally incapacitated, look forward to visiting with a guest or watching their favorite TV shows.

When people lose interest in life it is because they have nothing to look forward to; they become bored, even depressed. In these cases, it becomes even clearer that **goals are necessary for survival**.

Viktor Frankl, in his book *Man's Search for Meaning*, described this process among prisoners of World War II. Those who had family knew they had to survive to provide for these loved ones so they did what was necessary to continue. A professor, who was doing research that no one else was doing, knew that if he didn't survive valuable information for other people on the planet would be lost. He did what was necessary to withstand enormous difficulty, and he survived.

Those who had no goals, however, found no meaning in the daily struggle for life, psychologically gave up, and eventually died.

Studies have shown that teenagers who do not have long-range goals are more likely to fall into depression and even consider suicide. Hospital patients who have a great desire to get back to their "life business" are the ones who heal fastest.

I remember experiencing this process when I was only five years old. In Omaha, Nebraska, we did not have beaches but we did have a good many sand-pits which we used as beaches. On rare occasions, my parents would plan a day trip to LINOMA, a beach halfway between Lincoln and Omaha. As soon as my parents would announce such a trip was to happen, even if it was weeks away, we would all get excited. We would put on our bathing suits, get a beach ball and practice "beach" in the backyard. We would continually talk about what we would do that day, what we would eat, and we lived with great expectation. When the day was over, however, even though we'd had a wonderful time, it was as if the bottom had fallen out of our lives because we didn't have anything else to look forward to.

Look into your own life and you will find that when you look forward to something special in your future, you get excited about each day. You become creative about making arrangements and plans.

The important thing to remember is that you can create one goal after another so that when you achieve one you can have another in place. At that point, you will find yourself wanting to get involved, your life will be exciting and you discover meaning in your life.

Attitudes

The second factor that motivates is attitude, by that I mean the manner in which we view ourselves and our world. Some can look at a half-glass of water and say: "It's half full." Others see the same glass and say: "It's half empty." Both perceptions are valid, but they are different. We might say one is more positive and one more negative although these labels are also relative.

Our perception or the way we see things makes all the difference in the world when it comes to life experience. It is true that facts do not create reality. Reality is the way in which we perceive the facts.

Imagine two people shopping for a vase. Both have a clear idea of what they want. One finds the vase and is immediately excited. "It will look wonderful in the foyer," or "I can picture it in the center of the dining room table with flowers. I know the entire family will enjoy it!" This person buys the vase and returns home happy.

The second person, on the other hand, finds the vase and immediately checks the price. This individual thinks the vase would be perfect but believes the price is too high. After trying unsuccessfully to get the salesperson to lower the price, they become irritated and upset. "I'll find it somewhere else for a better price!" Unable to find the same vase for less or unable to find it elsewhere at all, the person becomes tired of running here and there, and angry about not having the vase, begins to think, "Business people are not fair with me," "Inflation is really bad," etc. Because of the viewpoint, this person is unhappy regardless of whether they get the vase!

So it is in your life. If you are able to see difficulty in your life as opportunity for growth, the difficulty will still be there but you will use it wisely and have a positive life experience. On the other hand, if you are a person who finds fault with everyone and everything, you will never be happy no matter what the circumstances.

How you look at yourself and the world around you reveals your attitude, and **it is your attitude that determines your experience of life**.

Free Choice

Human beings have been created with free choice. This characteristic, unique to that segment of the animal kingdom called "Homo Sapiens," has baffled the minds of philosophers over the centuries. It seems to be an obvious fact of our experience, yet it is impossible for anyone to explain.

In terms of the life mechanism, the ability we all have to make choices in our lives is the control factor. It is like the steering wheel of an automobile—move it one way and you get a certain result; move it another way and the result is different.

Because goals and attitudes determine the results we get in life, it is very important to consider how we make choices in these two important areas of daily living.

I believe there are only two categories of goals that make a difference in terms of the life mechanism. Either the goal is appropriate or it is inappropriate. Attitudes also fall into two categories: positive and negative. The choices we make in these two areas determine what the life experience will be.

Let me use an example. I had students who came into my General Music class with no music background at all, but they had a positive mental attitude. Their thought process was, "I don't know anything about music, but I am sure I can learn something in this class." I offered these students clearly defined and appropriate goals which they chose as their own. They motivated themselves to perform in a way that created a very satisfying life experience. These were the students who produced an "A." Please note, the "A" was the effect; the cause was the choice they made.

On the other hand, there were students who came to class with a completely different attitude. The very first day of class they sat with arms crossed, looking at the ceiling and tapping their feet as if to say: "Who needs this class?!" They were offered the same goals given the others, but they rejected them and set up their own—"I'm going to sleep in this class," "I'm going to read books," "I'm going to bug the teacher!"—not necessarily appropriate goals, but the students certainly had positive attitudes toward them. The result: they motivated themselves to act successfully in achieving their goals, but at the same time produced an "F." Again note, the "F" was the effect; the cause was the choice they made.

Generally when students with inappropriate goals or negative attitudes get an "F" and are forced to justify it, they point to the problem being "out there" someplace: "It's ...a dumb course, ...a bad teacher, ...the school system." All the reasons for their "F", generally interpreted as "failure," are projected outward. The fact is, the cause is within themselves, in the choices they have made. Until they realize that their life experience is the result of their choices, they will never understand that they are in control of their lives and will probably never suspect how much power they have to succeed.

This Life Mechanism works in exactly the same way in your life. If you choose appropriate goals and keep a positive attitude toward them, you can create a satisfying life experience. However, if you choose inappropriate goals or develop negative attitudes, you will create a life experience that will not be as satisfying. Choices do indeed create your own individual life experience.

The following is a summary outline of the Life Mechanism. This mechanism works for you everyday. It will give you a satisfying life experience if you make one set of choices, it will give you a dissatisfying life experience if you make a different set of choices. But it does work for you every day, all day.

The Life Mechanism

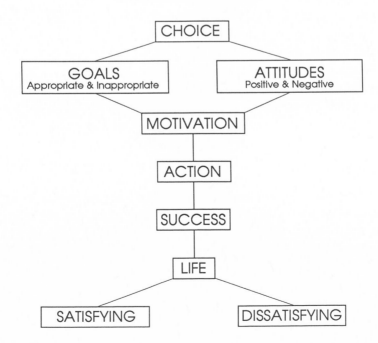

DIAGRAM 1

God and Faith

I would like to add two theological concepts to this description of the Life Mechanism to indicate how this material would fit into traditional theology. Theologians looking at this description would not be happy with the terminology because it is, essentially, secular. They would prefer, when talking about goals, to talk in terms of "God's will," and instead of talking about attitudes, they would prefer the term "Faith."

Theologians of all major religions teach that God wants for all of us that which will give us the highest fulfillment. Therefore, if one determines what is God's will and makes that their own personal goal, they can expect to have the fullness that they are destined to have here on this planet.

A similar comparison can be made with attitudes and faith. The saints and the holy people of organized religions from time immemorial were able to look at all life experience as opportunity for growth. They saw every experience of life in a positive light. That kind of mental attitude is a sign of what theologians refer to as "faith."

St. Lawrence, for example, was martyred by being burned alive on a grid-iron. In his biography we are told that in the midst of this experience he shouted out to the people who were executing him, "Turn me over, I'm done on this side!" Of course, people wonder how it could be that someone going through that kind of excruciating pain could joke. The explanation is very simple. St. Lawrence knew death was imminent, but he also believed that death was part of the fullness of life. With his attention focused on fully experiencing his death, the sensation of pain fell away.

The capacity to focus on choosing your experience of the moment is being taught today in stress centers all over the United States. One form of the skills being taught is bio-feedback. A patient who is wanting to control pain is attached by means of wires to a machine that beeps when it detects the nervous system activity that transmits pain. Patients concentrating on relaxing can cause the beeping to slow down. By becoming totally absorbed in relaxation, the patient can cause the experience of pain to diminish and disappear.

The principle is simple: choose positive thoughts and you will have a positive life experience.

In the chapters that follow we will examine this mechanism in detail. We will look first at the mind and the brain, and how they work. In chapters 3 and 4, we will explain how you can use visualization and affirmations to direct the mind and the brain. Chapter 5 explains how you can use mental skills to develop positive attitudes toward yourself, toward others and toward all life experience. Chapter 6 is devoted to skills needed to clarify goals so that you can plan your future life. The final chapter is a discussion of your unlimited potential and how you can activate it for a life that is full, productive and successful!!!

SUGGESTED ACTIVITIES

Ed. Note: Gather some blank paper and a pencil (remember, with a pencil you can never make a mistake) or your favorite art supplies and get yourself a quiet, comfortable location where you won't be disturbed for a least a few minutes. Spending some quality time with yourself, experimenting, even playing with these suggested activities, is guaranteed to start you on the way.

1. Write down one of your accomplishments. Go ahead and write it big and bold or draw a picture of it.
    – Describe your attitude toward this goal while you were working to achieve it. (If it will help, close your eyes and remember as much as you can of the journey toward this goal.)
    – How did you feel when you reached the goal?
    – Describe some of the obstacles you had to overcome to attain the goal.

2. Write down one objective that you are in the process of achieving at the present time.
    – Is your attitude toward the goal positive?
    – Do you have an easy time getting involved in activities that relate to its achievement?
    – If not, how can you change your attitude so that it will be easier for you to engage in activities related to its achievement?
    – How long will it take to achieve this goal?
    – What will be the next goal you plan to achieve?

3. Consider one past success (it may be the same one you used before, or a different one) and discuss it in terms of the Life Mechanism.
    – What choices did you make?
    – How did you articulate (or name) your goal?
    – How did you hold yourself present to your goal?
    – What was your attitude?

- How did you manifest your attitude? (It may be helpful here to remember times when you manifest an unhelpful attitude toward your goal. How did you catch yourself? What corrective actions did you take?)
- What actions did you have to take to achieve success?
- What was the final outcome? (How was it different than what you had envisioned?)
- What was the journey toward the goal like?

2

MIND/BRAIN

We are living in an exciting time. Until the recent past, people who wanted to learn about meditation had to go to some form of organized religion. Now, however, science is studying meditation. Fields like parapsychology and psychoneuroimmunology are creating a new language to explain what, in the past, has been called mystical phenomenon. Researchers are studying the experiences of holy people of all religions and demonstrating that the mystical experience (in science called psychic) is the property of every human being, and not limited to a chosen few. Historically, it is a time for us to study human beings in their non-material or spiritual dimension. Science and theology are coming together to form a union that is wonderful and unique.

History

In the early 1920s, Hans Berger began the basic research that led to the electroencephalograph. He knew that the human being is constantly emitting electrical energy, but he didn't know how much or what kind of energy it was. This energy field, also referred to as the aura, sometimes extends some distance from the body, sometimes it does not. Sometimes it is stronger, sometimes weaker; but it is always there.

In order to measure this energy at the brain level, Berger devised a system of taking small metal disks (approximately the size of a half dollar) and attaching them to a band that fit tightly around the head of his subject. Attached to these electrodes were wires that led to a machine that would measure the amount of electrical current passing through the wires. Because his subjects were always lying down, the readings that Berger obtained initially ranged between eight (8) and ten (10) cycles per second.

One day, a subject who was lying on a cot got up to get a glass of water with the electrodes still attached. The person doing the monitoring realized that after the subject got up from the cot, the brain frequencies were going higher than 12 cycles.

This phenomena precipitated a whole new set of experiments in which the subjects did the kind of things that you and I do in our normal waking state. Berger then realized that, when functioning during an average day, human beings generated between 14 and 28 cycles of energy per second. In order to distinguish between these two areas he called the first area "Alpha," the first letter of the Greek alphabet, because he found it first. The second he referred to as "Beta."

Since that time researchers have discovered two others areas of brain functioning. One that goes down to 4 cycles is referred to as "Theta" and a fourth that goes down to near 0 which is referred to as "Delta."

In order for an average person to function normally, it is important that a certain amount of time be spent in the upper brain frequencies as well as in the lower brain frequencies every 24 hours. This balancing usually takes place during sleep. At night, an individual begins to feel tired as the brain frequencies slow down. Normally, as the person gets more and more relaxed, the brain frequencies lower to 12 or less. When the person lets go of conscious awareness, sleep occurs. The brain frequencies then move all the way down to Delta, then back up again into Alpha and down again (but not quite so deep), then up again (a little bit higher), forming an upward

Brain Frequency Patterns

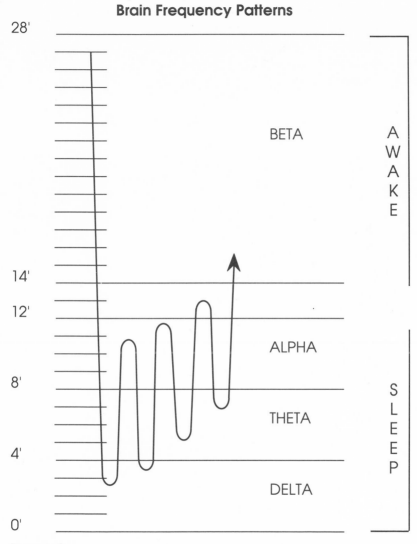

DIAGRAM 2

pattern until, in the morning, the brain frequencies speed up beyond 14 cycles and the person awakens.

Since we don't want to go into the entire history of the electroencephalogram here, let it suffice to distinguish clearly the lower brain frequencies from the higher ones. For most of us who are lay people, in terms of this information, we know the upper level brain frequencies (14-28) as "conscious" awareness and the lower level brain frequencies (Delta, Theta, and Alpha) as "subconscious" awareness.

Before going into the practical application of this theory let us first clarify a distinction between brain and mind.

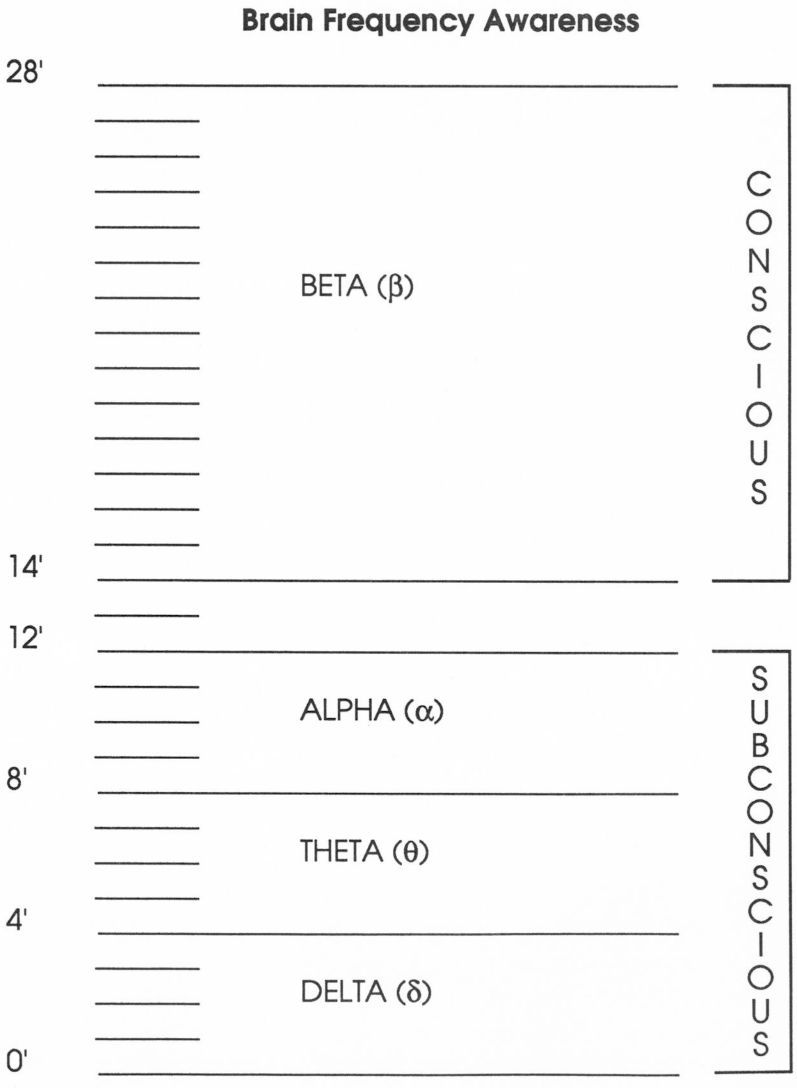

Brain Frequency Awareness

Diagram 3

Brain

The **brain** is the physical organ located directly below the cranium—it is a machine. The **mind**, on the other hand, is the energy that makes the brain work. If we were to use the comparison of a light bulb, we could refer to the bulb as the brain and the electricity that makes the bulb glow as the mind.

The brain is, perhaps, the most important organ in the body because it controls the other parts. At this very moment, the brain is sending messages to your lungs which keep them functioning. It tells your heart to beat; it tells your eyelids to blink; it keeps your body temperature even, the metabolism going, etc.

An important fact about the brain is that it is made up of cells that do not reproduce. For example, when you cut your finger skin cells are destroyed. Immediately, the blood begins to coagulate and form a protective cover so that the skin cells can go to work mending the wound. It takes awhile but, eventually, the skin cells reproduce a sufficient number of cells to cover the area perfectly. The new cells then push the scab away and you have a perfect repair job.

Most people do not understand that this reproductive process is absent in the brain. Nor do they realize that taking drugs of any kind, including alcohol, to the point of feeling "high" causes destruction of brain cells. Once brain cells are destroyed, they will never be revived or replaced. Misuse of drugs and alcohol is one way of systematically crippling the brain and creating a mentally limited human being.

As a child growing up in Omaha I experienced a good deal of drinking. In the Polish neighborhood where we lived, there were three taverns on one corner: Micek's, Zigurski's and the Idle Hour. On Saturday night that corner was the entertainment center of the community!

You can imagine that in this kind of community there were alcoholic people. I remember one family whose son was alcoholic. He began drinking in high school and was a confirmed alcoholic by the time he graduated from college. In the following years he married and fathered seven children. He also became completely incapacitated by alcohol. His wife had to get a job to provide for the family. One day she returned home and found her husband in the living room with their youngest child, a five-year-old girl. He had taken lighter fluid from the charcoal burner in the back yard and had sprayed the child. As the mother walked into the living room, she heard him saying, "You tell me where the booze is or I'm gonna light you!" He had matches in his hand. The wife told her husband, "Honey, I love you, but you have to go."

She got a room for him and his father began to send him an allowance which, of course, he used for drinking. He eventually left the room to live in an abandoned automobile. He drank enough to kill off the brain cells that keep the heart going and he dropped dead. This tragic story is all too common in our society.

If we as human beings want to live a full life we must pick up the responsibility of caring for our brains and teach brain hygiene to our children.

Besides being made up of very special cells, the brain also functions like a huge computer with virtually unlimited capacity. Your brain has stored and continues to store every bit of information with which you have come in contact from the earliest days of your existence to the present moment. Every book you've read, every person you've met, every life experience—all of it is recorded in great detail. Even more exciting is the fact that *you can retrieve this information* if you know how. For most of us, having this capacity is like having a computer in our homes which, if we have not learned to use it, just sits there.

Information stored in the brain can be accessed in many ways. One means is electrical current. By taking an electrode, a metal rod carrying an electrical current of about 10 cycles per second, and touching it to the brain, the subject can get immediate recall of the information stored on those cells. Researchers obtained this information by working with patients who had to undergo brain surgery. By administering only local anesthetic, they were able to communicate with the patient during the operation when the cranium was open and the brain exposed. They would touch the brain with the electrode and ask the patient what was being experienced. The images were recorded. Whenever the electrode touched the same area, the experience recalled by the patient was always the same. Although effective, this technique is not practical. You cannot, for example, run to the operating room every time you lose your car keys in order to find out where they are!!!

Another method of retrieving information is the use of drugs, which we have already mentioned. Drugs, however, activate many parts of the brain randomly. In some cases, while a drug may be known to activate one part of the brain, it may simultaneously be damaging another part. Because this random activation may be unrelated, the subject can get the experience of hallucinating and may or may not be able to later recall the information retrieved. Drugs as a method of retrieval are not very practical either.

A third method is hypnosis. By getting a person very relaxed, a skilled technician can help them activate the energy in the brain at a specific point and recall detailed information that has been stored. Law enforcement agencies are using this technique with people who have been at the scene of a crime but who cannot, consciously, recall the details. Under hypnosis, however, they can often recall details of facial features, clothing, license plate numbers, and so on. It is interesting to note that only a few years ago the Supreme Court ruled that information obtained through hypnosis can be used in a court of law.

A fourth method of obtaining information from the brain is called meditation. Meditation can be considered the theological term and "altered states of consciousness" the scientific term for the same basic human experience. It is important to note that although meditation is an "altered state" of consciousness—not all "altered states" are meditation. (Science, for instance, refers to hypnosis as an altered state of consciousness.) By learning to relax mentally and physically so that brain frequencies can be lowered, people can use the mind to activate the brain at specific points in order to recall specific information. This technique is not only possible but very practical since it can be learned by anyone!

Mind

We have briefly discussed some important facts regarding the brain; let us turn our attention now to the mind.

The mind is completely different than the brain. It is the energy that activates the brain. In theological terms the mind might be referred to as "soul" or "spirit."

Although the mind is non-material and more intangible, nonetheless, science is researching this dimension of human beings. One important fact that has emerged is that when the brain functions at frequencies below 12 cycles, the mind can be freed of all limits (even the limits of time and space). As early as 1900, Joseph Conrad of England commented, "The mind is capable of anything—because everything is in it, all the past as well as all the future." This means that when the brain frequencies are in Alpha or lower, the mind can move frontwards or backwards in time and from one place on the planet to any other place in the Universe.

This information may begin to sound like science fiction. However, the facts demonstrate that many people receive information about the future in dreams. Perhaps, you have also had this kind of experience. As I have lectured throughout the country and abroad, I have found it a common occurrence among people to have experienced pre-cognitive dreams. When I was preparing for lecturing and teaching in the area of meditation and altered states of consciousness, I spent one semester in Jerusalem where I examined in detail the scripture passages that spoke of dreams and visions. These experiences are common in the Bible.

In our culture, unfortunately, most of us have been taught to disregard dreams as "occult" instead of viewing them as a way of communicating with higher consciousness. Even in the seminary we were warned to avoid dealing with dreams. In other cultures, however, children are taught to remember dreams as soon as they can talk. In these cultures dreams are an important aid for setting personal goals and for solving problems.

Today attitudes toward dreams and meditation are changing drastically. Spiritual directors are now being trained to teach methods of recalling and using dreams for life planning and problem solving. Dreams are again being used to help people listen to a source of deeper wisdom.

Meditation

As we said previously, your brain holds all of the information that you come in touch with every day but most of that information is held in the subconscious mind. Although you may not be consciously aware of it, the sum total of all the information you have stored determines the kind of person you are. In other words, the way you function in your normal waking state is due entirely to the information that has been recorded on your brain at the subconscious level. The subconscious is the cause, the way you function is the effect. That

A Relational View

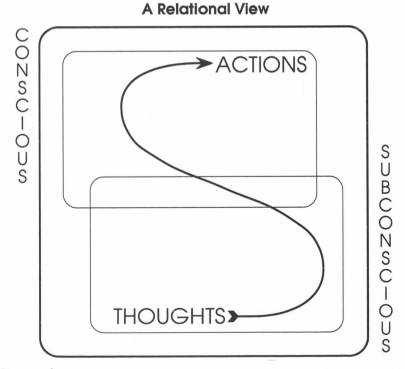

DIAGRAM 4

means if you want to change anything in your life the least effective place for you to go is the conscious mind.

Have you ever met anyone who has stopped smoking, and then stopped again, and still needs to stop? Or maybe closer to home, do you know anyone who has ever been on a diet, then another diet, and still needs a diet? If you ask any of these people if they want to change, they answer "Yes," and they mean it! Then why is it that they have such a difficult time changing their behavior? The reason is that they have put a very powerful program in their brain at the subconscious level. It is the sub-conscious program that projects itself into their

Images Affect Actions

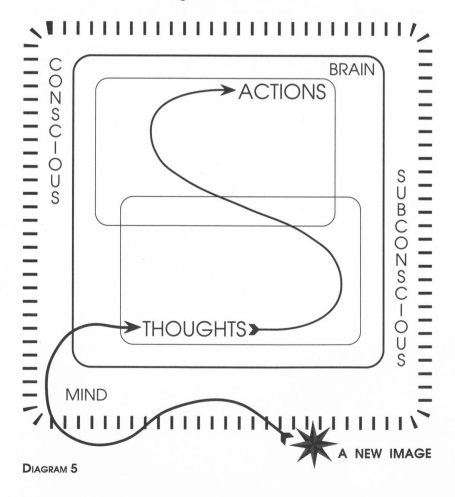

DIAGRAM 5

conscious life. We are, indeed, the sum total of all the thoughts we have gathered throughout our lives.

The question then is, how can I go about changing my life? The answer is simple. **Create images with the mind** that will reflect the way you want to be in the future. Those images will get **impressed on the brain** and, if they are repeated over and over again, they will become part of the subconscious mind. Once that happens your **behavior will change.**

This process of change can take place very quickly. Years ago, I knew a Friar professor who smoked more cigarettes than any person I have ever known. (Ironically, his name was Blaze.) As he got older, doctors told him to give up smoking or prepare to give up his life because his heart could no longer take the stress. He told them he had tried to stop over and over again, but had never been successful. One doctor recommended a personal friend who was also an M.D. and a hypnotist. Blaze made the trip to Chicago and arrived at the doctor's office to find that the doctor dealt with two people at a time. Blaze was paired off with a businessman who had also come in from out of town. When they got into the doctor's office they were seated in comfortable recliner chairs and the doctor assisted them into a very relaxed state. He had them imagine times when they would normally be smoking and then had them visualize the cigarettes disappearing so that the picture would not include cigarettes. When having a cup of coffee at breakfast, for example, they were asked to imagine one hand on the coffee cup and the other hand resting comfortably on the table or on their lap. They were asked to visualize being at the table eating the normal amounts of food and seeing themselves in every other way being happy and healthy. The doctor also helped them with some positive affirmations relating to clean lungs and easy breathing.

After about 20 minutes the doctor said, "Gentlemen the interview is over." The two men opened their eyes and looked at each other as if to say, "Is that all there is?"

When they got into the hallway, the businessman told Blaze, "I am not leaving town until I find out if this thing works. I think we both got took!" Blaze was in agreement and so they decided to dine together. Before the meal, when they were having a drink, the businessman asked Blaze, "Would you like to have a cigarette?" Blaze answered, "No, thank you." When they finished their meal, Blaze asked the businessman, "Would you like a cigarette?" and the businessman answered, "No, thank you." They had indeed lost their desire for cigarettes.

If you know the theory, the process is very logical. The hypnotist is skilled at helping the individual use the mind to create images that impress new information on the brain with such intensity that it becomes part of the subconscious mind. Once that happens, it has an immediate effect on the way the individual functions. (See Diagram 5)

Hypnosis is not the only way to impress new information on the brain. It is also possible to teach individuals to relax mentally and physically so they can lower their brain frequencies at will. While in that relaxed state they can direct their own thought process. By creating new images with the mind and impressing them on the brain at the subconscious level, they can change any aspect of their lives.

This process of impressing new information on brain cells at the subconscious level can be referred to as "meditation." This skill has been recommended by all major religions over the centuries. They have said that if you want to take total control of your life you must learn to meditate.

Fill your mind with good, healthy, wholesome, positive thoughts, and impress those images on the brain. They will get into the subconscious and create a good, healthy, wholesome, positive life experience.

The opposite is also true. Fill your mind with sick, negative, limiting, violent thoughts and you will have a sick, negative, limiting and violent life. What we are talking about here are the most basic laws of cause and effect.

Universal Law

If you hold a pencil in front of you and let go, it will fall to the floor. The reason for this phenomenon is the law of gravity. This law applies to all physical objects on the planet—it works without exception all day, every day.

There are similar laws that govern human actions—laws that are just as immutable and which apply across the board. If you choose a goal that is good for you, you will have a positive effect—you will never change that fact. The opposite is also true, if you choose to do something that is not good for you, you will achieve a negative result—you will not change that law either.

The same is true of attitudes. If you have a positive attitude, even when life is difficult or painful, you will have a positive life experience. Similarly, when life deals you a straight flush and everything seems to be falling into place but you have a negative attitude, you will be unhappy. The law is clear—appropriate goals + positive attitudes = full living. Inappropriate goals + negative attitudes = limited life experience.

Applications

This material is being put to practical use in a number of fields today. Two fields putting major emphasis on this practical application are healing and education.

Some years ago, a man by the name of Jose Silva created a practical program to train people to use the mind-brain mechanism. O. Carl Simonton and Stephanie M. Simonton, applied this material to cancer. In the book, *Getting Well Again*, they described in detail the images their patients used to promote healing of terminal cancer. They had outstanding success and are both now recognized as international authorities. Their insights were shared with Dr. Bernie Siegel, who applied these techniques to healing all illness. His book, *Love, Medicine and Miracles*, contains a review of an AIDS patient who was able to reactivate his immune system by using relaxation and visualization. A whole new science called psychoneuroimmunology is emerging, proving that positive thoughts stimulate the immune system while negative thoughts deactivate the immune system.

The other field in which meditation is being applied is education. In 1979 two women, Ostrander and Schroeder, traveled behind the Iron Curtain. In Bulgaria they found a professor by the name of Dr. Georgi Lozanov who was applying these techniques to teaching. By activating right and left brain and using altered states of consciousness, Dr. Lozanov was able to accelerate the learning process up to seven times what we know in traditional classrooms here in the United States.

These two women have described Dr. Lozanov's techniques in the book titled, *Superlearning*. Since that time, Dr. Lozanov's work has become known throughout the world—his system of teaching is called Suggestopedia. As more and more educators are trained in this field, Lozanov Institutes are appearing all over the world. Here in the United States professional educators have created the Society for Accelerative Learning Techniques (SALT) and are doing continuing research on the methodology. Their findings have been published in the SALT *Journal*. In Australia another organization exists called the Accelerative Learning Society of Australia (ALSA) with headquarters in Adelaide. Similar professional associations exist around the world.

At the University of Houston, Suggestopedia is the only method being used to teach foreign language. With this approach, students can learn to use a foreign language in one week. The University, of course, is attracting students from all over the country especially businessmen seeking language skills for international business.

Relaxation and visualization are also being applied in the sports arena. Not only individual athletes but entire clubs are being given training in these mental disciplines with outstanding results. Special reports have been done on the positive results acquired by their use in the last two Olympic competitions.

Applications for Life

The scientific developments regarding mind and brain in the fields of health and education are exciting indeed. Our major concern in this book, however, is the application of this material in your daily life.

Living in today's world is truly a challenge. Enormous amounts of negativity bombard the communication and entertainment media. Crowded living conditions, environmental pollution, economic stress, volatile family situations and co-dependency issues all offer their own challenges. But the premises here are:

➠ We all have free will and can make choices
    to shape our lives any way we wish, and

➠ We all have an unlimited potential
    which we can activate
    by skillful use of the mind and the brain.

In the pages that follow, we will move through a thought process that will explain what you can do to take control of your life. By taking control of your mind you can choose the goals and attitudes that can make your life experience consistently positive, meaningful and enjoyable.

SUGGESTED ACTIVITIES

It is almost impossible to overstate the value of relaxation. Relaxation has immeasurable value whether you desire to diminish the effects of stress in your life or you desire to sleep better at night. Relaxation can literally help you breathe easier, get more oxygen flowing through your system, lower your blood pressure and much more.

1. Get into a comfortable position, either sitting or reclining. If you choose to sit in a chair, have both your feet flat on the floor. If you choose to lie down, let your arms rest at your side.

    a. With your eyes closed, tell yourself that as you slowly count backwards from 50 to 1 you will become more and more relaxed.

    b. Stay with your state of relaxation for a few moments. Notice how your body feels. With your mind very still, focus on your intentions for the day, or on your accomplishments.

    c. When you are ready, particularly if you are going into your day's activities, count back up from 1 to 50. Tell yourself as you slowly count forward that you are becoming more and more alert and filled with energy.

2. There is an approach to relaxation that will work for everyone. The more you use it, the easier and more automatic it will become. For some who have found the method described above helpful, they tell of reaching a point where they simply need to say to themselves in a tense situation "50-40-30-20-10-Relaxed," and they will find their perspective transformed. The reverse is also true when they need more energy for a situation. If the above method is not the approach most helpful for you, Experiment! until you discover what is best for you.

    • Let your body help you. Ask your toes to relax, your feet to relax, etc., until you reach the top of your head.

    • Let nature help you. Picture yourself standing under a soft, warm waterfall that is bringing everything you need into your life. As the water washes over you, let it bring you relaxation.

- Let the ongoing and natural process of your breathing help you. Breathe in health and harmony, breathe out tension.

3. Reading can be a relaxing activity. For some people, reading at the end of the day will stir their mind until they can't easily sleep for all the ideas running around; for others, it is the ideal way to implant new ideas deeply while they are relaxing and preparing for sleep. Knowing yourself will help you determine when to read what kind of material. The following is a short list (see References for more) of resources that focus on applications of brain/mind research to key disciplines

   Getting Well Again by O. Carl & Stephanie Simonton
   Love, Medicine and Miracles by Bernie Siegel, M.D.
   Silva Mind Control Method by Jose Silva
   Super Immunity by Paul Pearsall, Ph.D.
   Superlearning by Ostrander and Schroeder
   You Can Heal Your Life by Louise L. Hay

4. Listening to audio tapes can be a helpful aid in relaxation. You may choose to record your own voice counting down from 50 to 1. *Basic Relaxation* by Therese Ann Coddington (see References) used on a regular basis will soon help you relax at will.

5. Seeking encounters with the mind/brain, mind/body connections through practical applications will quickly bring clarity to the information shared in this chapter.
   - Get information from your local telephone directory for the Silva Method of Mind Development and schedule yourself into a class. If you want to improve your athletic skills look into the Silva Star Athlete Program.
   - If you are an educator, check into teacher training in Suggestopedia.
   - If you are interested in language, contact the University of Houston about their programs or organizations that use their methods.

Testing these approaches with others who share like objectives can provide valuable reflection, shorten the learning curve and sustain and support your process.

3

IMAGES AND VISUALIZATION

Most of us have come to think of communication as verbal (using words). This method is common to most everyone, but it is not the only possibility. Images are another method of communication which, at times, can be more effective; in fact, in some cases, images are the only way to successfully communicate.

Suppose you have just purchased a beautiful painting for your living room. You are on the phone talking to a friend and you try to convey the experience of the picture by talking about it and describing some details. No matter what you say, you soon realize that the other person is not getting the complete idea so you invite your friend to come to the house. Only when you both stand in front of the picture do you know that the other person even has the possibility of the same experience of the painting.

The language of the mind is images, and the problems that arise from trying to describe a picture verbally will be the same problems encountered when you try to describe any mental image in words. Using words to describe mental images is not only difficult, in many cases it is impossible. This is why people misunderstand each other when they are having a conversation. It is not that they are necessarily unclear in the language they use, but rather that it is impossible to completely transfer the images of the mind through the medium of words.

Images and the Senses

When talking about mental "images" I mean to imply experiences of all of the senses—taste, smell, sight, hearing and feeling. For example, you have the ability to recall not only what chocolate tastes like but you can mentally distinguish between tastes of different kinds of chocolate. For that reason, you may prefer one kind of candy to another or one brand of chocolate topping over another. Some people are so skilled they can imagine several tastes in combination. These people may put their talent to work becoming fine chefs.

In much the same way, you can imagine several odors and mentally compare them. It is this talent that allows you to distinguish and identify different colognes or perfumes.

Images that relate to sight allow you to look at a small piece of material and imagine what an entire wall would look like or to mentally put a whole room together. Interior designers are good at this kind of visualization.

Handel, when asked about creating the *"Alleluia Chorus,"* explained that he composed none of it. He said, "I heard the angels singing," and all he did was transcribe the sound to paper. You use this same talent recalling a favorite song or the sound of the sea.

Feelings also can be imaged. A couple, for example, have a favorite song which was being played when they first met. Every time they hear the song, they can recall what they felt when they were young lovers.

Each of these ways of imaging are common to everyone and used daily. It is these human experiences I refer to when I use the words "visualization" or "mental images."

Characteristics of Images

There are several characteristics of images that make them valuable especially in altered states of consciousness or meditation.

First of all, images are *produced in an instant*. It takes only a few seconds to recall or create a mental image. Suppose you are looking for the solution to a problem. You have been considering several alternatives for some time. All of a sudden, the correct choice becomes clear. It's as if a light bulb goes on; you "see" the situation clearly and are able to make a choice easily. The whole process takes only a few seconds.

Another important characteristic of images is that they *contain enormous detail* even if you are not conscious of it! Recall a wedding ceremony or a ball game you have experienced in the past. The whole scene comes back immediately in all its detail. As you focus on one aspect of the event after another you can describe a great many details because it is all in your mental picture.

A third unique characteristic of images is that they are a *universal language*. No matter where you go on the planet, everyone reads pictures. For that reason restrooms, phone booths, restaurants, road signs, are all being identified by stylized pictures. Museums display paintings, carvings, and sculpture from prehistoric times to the present and from places all over the world. Everyone, no matter what their language, can look at these images and appreciate them.

Images and Science

With all the study of mind and brain taking place in the academic world there is a great deal of interest among scientists to understand and explain the connection between the body and the mind (spirit). For that reason, whole new sciences are coming into existence.

Psychophysiology and Neuro-Linguistic Programming have clearly identified a relationship between eye movements and mental functions. Nine distinct positions of the eyes are:

	Left (memory of)	**Center**	**Right** (creative)
Upper	sights	odors	sights
Horizontal	sounds	synthesizing	sounds
Lower	emotional experiences	tastes	physical sensations

Eyes Left

When you focus your eyes to the upper left, you activate memory of sight images.

When you focus at the horizontal left, you trigger memory of sound.

When your eyes are focused downward and left, you trigger memory of emotional experiences or feelings.

Eyes Center

Focusing upward center you stimulate memory of odors.

Focusing downward center stimulates memory of tastes.

Focusing horizontally and to the center synthesizes all of the senses.

Eyes Right

Focusing upward but to the right activates creative images of sight.

Focusing horizontally right activates creative image of sound.

Focusing downward right triggers memory of physical sensations or feelings.

You may ask: "What is the practicality of this?" If you are a parent, teacher, or employer and you want to know where your child, student or employee has been the night before, watch where their eyes focus as they answer your questions. If they have a tendency to look to the upper left while communicating they are recalling facts. If, however, they are focusing to the upper right while they speak, you know they are stimulating their creative imagination.

This information can also be used effectively to stimulate certain kinds of mental activity. For example, if you want to recall some particular tastes, focus downward center first and then pay attention to what happens in your memory. These skills can be taught by parents and teachers who can in turn aid youngsters in developing creative visualization and image memory.

Parapsychology has begun to describe the connection between the brain and mind as a truly efficient, effective team. The mind creates information which the brain stores and, when properly stimulated, the brain will give the information back to the mind. One of the applied techniques for education is called the "George Concept." In this approach, students are taught to communicate to their sub-conscious minds as if they were talking to another person called George. "George" then becomes a psychological button that students can use when they wish to get information from the brain which is stored at the sub-conscious level. Visualizing is, of course, the most effective way to communicate with "George."

Although mind and brain make a very successful team, remember that there are differences between them. The mind can distinguish images created by the physical senses from those sometimes referred to as "synthetic" which are created by the mind alone. The brain on the other hand, functions strictly as a machine; it does not know if the information it receives is synthetic or not. It simply takes in all information and processes it.

Let me suggest a brief exercise. As you read these lines, imagine a large, fresh, juicy lemon on a plate resting on your lap. (Pause after each sentence, and with your eyes closed create a detailed mental picture.) Imagine that you have a knife in one hand and the lemon in the other. Now picture yourself cutting the lemon and imagine the scent of lemon reaching your nostrils while the juice flows onto the plate. See yourself picking up the lemon in your hand, squeezing it gently so that the cut edge is filled with juice. Now mentally bring it to your face and draw your tongue across the lemon picking up the juice and feeling the texture of the lemon.

What shape is your face in? Did you feel yourself salivating during this exercise? Did you feel a pull on both sides of your jaw as you imagined the tart taste? Please note that there is no lemon present at all but the body reacts as if there is one because the mind has visualized it. The brain has processed the information, and the body responds accordingly.

Going a step further, psychoneuroimmunology has discovered that the brain can communicate with the mind present in the immune system and the mind in the immune system can communicate with the brain.

One experiment was done to show how images affect the immune system. A random group of individuals was asked to donate blood samples so that a T cell count could be obtained. (The T cell is a lymphocyte in our blood system that defends the body against viruses and bacteria.) The subjects then sat in a room for one-half hour viewing pictures that were positive— scenes of nature, a mother holding an infant, children at play. After the half-hour, samples of blood were taken a second time. These samples showed a significant rise in the T cell count. The same subjects then returned to the projection room but this time were shown a half-hour of negative images—pictures of Auschwitz, starving people in Africa, battered women and children. After this session, blood samples were taken again and the T cell count was found to be significantly lower.

A principle derived from this research can be stated as follows: You cannot fool around with the mind and the brain! Use them in a positive way and you will obtain positive results; use them in a negative way and you will get negative results.

Practical applications of the above might be: expose yourself only to TV shows that present positive images to stimulate your immune system for better health—or read only books and magazines that contain positive images and ideas—or get into the habit of talking about the good things that are happening in your life and in the world.

Teilhard de Chardin, a paleontologist, explained the power of the mind and the brain on the external world when he stated that for any change to happen in the universe, it is necessary only that one person have a thought. Once a sufficient amount of time passes, that thought will materialize.

Let me share with you an example that was very powerful in my own life. When I was a child, my Mother's only night out was Friday. On that evening, Dad stayed home to take care of the younger children and Mom went off to the movies. As we got older, my brother, Jack, and I were frequently allowed to go to the theater with her.

On one of these occasions, when I was only 10 or 11 years old, we went to see the movie *"Luxury Liner."* That movie made a strong impression on me. I was able to mentally put myself on the ship and actually be one of the characters portrayed on the screen.

One scene, in particular, I remember with great clarity. Jane Powell, a fine vocalist and the star of the film, was the one I related to in a romantic way. At one point in the story, she was dressed in a beautiful evening gown and escorted to the rail of the elegant ship by a gentleman in a black tuxedo. The camera was behind them as they leaned on the rail watching the sea go by. A beautiful Caribbean moon illuminated the scene. Mentally, I became the young man standing next to Jane Powell.

Years later when I was teaching high school as a friar-priest, Mr. & Mrs. Dell (who had a son in my class) organized a group from the school to take a one-week cruise from New York to Nassau aboard a new ship called the *Oceanic*. There were about 16 of us in the group: the principal of the school, several teachers, some parents, a few students, friends, my aunt, two uncles and myself.

We were having a wonderful time, especially in the evenings. After dinner, the entire group went to the lounge at the rear of the ship for traditional kinds of dancing with the older members of the group. About midnight, we walked the "old timers" to their cabins and went to another lounge at the front of the ship where more contemporary dance music was being played. At 2 a.m. when this lounge closed, we gathered in the "Crow's Nest" on the upper deck for pizza and more dancing.

Ever since childhood I had enjoyed dancing, was later able to take lessons and eventually performed on the stage. This regular nightly routine aboard the *Oceanic* was a rare oppor-tunity for me as a priest, and I was on the dance floor all night long.

From the moment we boarded the ship, I was introducing myself (and being introduced) as "Father Justin" even though I was wearing a suit and tie. The young women, especially those with whom I was dancing every evening, thought we were playing a game and began to introduce themselves as "Sister Mary," "Sister Jean," etc.

Each night we had the same entertainment schedule. After several days I had used all my dress shirts and had to put on my black suit and roman collar for dinner. When I walked into the dining room there was a hush. People stared and a Jewish couple sitting near my Uncle Pete tugged at his coat and commented: "He really is a priest!"

After dinner we eventually worked our way to the Crow's Nest. When I walked in, several young ladies did a double take at my collar and looked with opened mouths—one dropped her drink all over the floor!

Later on the dance floor my partner asked, "Do you say Mass and hear confessions?"

"Yes," I answered.

She then asked if I could hear her confession. "Of course," I replied, "When would you like to get together?"

"How about now?" she asked.

"Fine," I responded.

We left the lounge and stepped out onto the deck. It was a beautiful evening and as we leaned on the rail watching the sea move by we looked up at a full moon. At that moment, the image of the movie from my childhood came back. IT WAS HAPPENING! There I was in a black suit with this beautiful woman. It was a powerful and, in some ways a frightening experience.

(Just to finish this story, I did hear her confession and when she finished she was in tears—so was I. We embraced and went back to the party. She was quick to tell others: "He really is a priest. He heard my confession!" Needless to say, I was back at the railing again and again during the course of the evening. I began to think: "If I had known the priesthood was going to be this good, I would have joined earlier!")

The mind (using images) is a powerful instrument for creating reality. Be very careful what you put into your mind and therefore your brain, for what you enter will become your reality.

Visualization and Your Health

At present, more and more is being written about visualization and its effect on health and healing. A recent research project done by the Medical School of the University of California, San Francisco, was reported in the *Brain / Mind Bulletin:* asthmatics who used visualization techniques to travel through their bodies to help troubled cells needed less medication than control patients.

Elmer Green in his book *Beyond Biofeedback* quoted Dr. Will J. Erwood who said, "The body will do what you tell it, if you learn how to tell it. The way of telling it involves quietness plus a visualization of what you want the body to do." Elmer Green himself described how he was able to dissolve calcium deposits in his shoulder by using visualization.

Suggesting Images to Others

Suggesting images to others can have effective results also but you must remember that, although you have direct control of yourself and your thought process, you do not have direct control over the thought process of others. You can suggest images to others, but they are always free to accept or reject them. If they accept the images, the thoughts can influence their lives.

Theater owners across the country have repeated the image of popcorn, not only visually but also with sounds, odors and colorful containers. After years of repeating the suggestion, most people preparing to watch a movie automatically desire and purchase popcorn, even if they are watching movies at home.

Some of these suggestions can be a matter of life and health. Doctors, nurses and other health care professionals, for example, can have an influence on patients by the images they project. I once knew a nurse, a graduate of my classes, who consciously reflected positive images to her patients. She was constantly directing their attention to the positive gains made, even if those gains were minimal. She daily suggested that they were getting better and better. As a result, it was a known fact that the patients in her department healed more quickly.

Teachers, too, can project images that have a lasting impact on the lives of their students. Suggestopedia practitioners have carefully documented the fact that teachers who state over and over again that learning is easy and fun actually create that experience in the classroom for their students.

The same is true of the kind of images that the students project toward the teachers. Years ago, I read the book *Teaching As a Subversive Activity* in which the author, Neil Postman, suggested that students who wanted to be happier in school project more positive images toward the teacher. One year, I suggested this procedure to my class as an experiment. The students followed up and chose to work on a teacher they disliked to see if their projected thought process could have an effect. They were dealing with an English teacher who had a negative attitude and who was very demanding. Every time the teacher created a positive experience in the class, these students were careful to reflect their approval by a comment in the hallway or at lunchtime. They did extra little things like remembering the teacher's birthday with a meaningful gift and offered honest compliments whenever they could. The teacher's image of the class began to change and to their great amazement the relationship between the students and this teacher became not only workable but even pleasant. It was interesting, in this particular experiment, that the teacher did not change her attitude or behavior in other English classes.

Visualization is by far the most powerful means of making changes in human beings because the language of the mind and brain is images.

SUGGESTED ACTIVITIES

1. Stop! Notice the images you are impressing on your brain right now. What are you taking in through your sense of sight? your sense of smell? through touch and taste? What are you feeling?
   • Just stopping to notice these things several times in a day will help you consciously screen the images you are letting in.

2. Get together with a friend or group of friends to practice imaging. Invite everyone to bring at least one picture from a magazine or newspaper. Pair off and using words only, create the image of your picture in the mind of your partner. Describe it using as much detail as you can. When you have finished, give the other person a moment to consolidate their image, then show them the picture.
   a. How close was their image to the picture you were describing? Can you discern some of the words that were very differently interpreted?
   b. Now trade roles and have your partner describe their picture to you. Reflect on what you learned.
   c. The whole group may want to reflect at this point, or if you have the time, it is fun to switch partners and describe the same picture to a different person.

3. Practice visualization by picturing in your mind each morning the things you know you want to achieve that day. Picturing in your mind the finished product may even show you how the job is going to get done. Don't forget to reflect at the end of the day on both your visualization and your success. You might not notice how much you can accomplish without really trying!

4. Make an effort to notice, remember and talk about the good things that are going on in your life. Then notice how good you begin to feel!

5. For more information on visualization you may want to read *Creative Visualization* by Shakti Gawain, *How to Use Your Power of Visualization* by Emily Lyons, or *Creative Visualization* by Ronald Shone.

4

AFFIRMATIONS

 Although the most effective method of putting new information on brain cells is by means of images, it is possible to get effective results by using affirmations.

Definition and Explanation

Affirmations are short positive statements that describe some specific result. Such statements do not describe situations as they are, but as you intend them to be. They are articulated in the present tense because now is the moment of intention.

Suppose you are a disorganized person and you would like to become more organized. You might compose an affirmation like this: "I am always organized in everything I do." Or if you are in the habit of being late for appointments and are interested in changing that behavior, you might use an affirmation like the following: "I am always 5 minutes early for my appointments."

By using statements like these over and over again, you can effectively put new information in your brain by impressing it at the subconscious level of the mind, which will automatically direct you to produce the result described in the affirmation.

Actually, affirmations are verbal symbols for identifying and recalling mental images. The closer you can come to calling forth an image (something you can picture) through your affirmation, the more powerful it can become. For example, when you use the affirmation, "I am always organized in everything I do," it may be the verbal symbol for picturing your desk at work being neat and clean, or for picturing your living space attractive and orderly. You can extend the power of the affirmation by saying, "I have a neat and clean desk at the end of every day."

As stated in the previous chapter on visualization, you can create mental images related to all the senses—sight, smell, touch, taste and hearing. Affirmations can be directed to recalling specific images in any or all of these areas.

Suppose you are interested in adding to or subtracting from your present body weight. You can not only picture yourself at that ideal weight but you can create a mental image of how you feel. These feelings can be recalled in an affirmation in this way: "I feel wonderful and happy at my ideal weight of 150 lbs."

Or suppose the doctor wants you to correct your diet by adding more fruits and vegetables. The problem is that at present you do not have a taste for these foods. By using an affirmation like: "I enjoy the taste of fruits and vegetables and feel totally satisfied after eating them," you can change your tastes and produce a feeling of satisfaction every time you eat these foods. The same process can be used to change the way you respond to certain odors, sounds or physical sensations.

History

Affirmations are nothing new; they have been used successfully from time immemorial. In the Old Testament (Isaiah 55:10-11) the "word" is described as a powerful force:

> For as the rain and the snow come down from heaven and return not thither but water the earth, making it bring forth and sprout, giving seed to the sower and bread to the eater, so shall my word be that goes forth from my mouth; it shall not return to me empty, but it shall accomplish that which I propose and prosper in the thing for which I sent it.

The understanding of this reality is the basis for the ancient practice of affirmations in monasteries from very early times right up to the present. When I entered the Franciscan Order in 1954, we were taught to create short prayers that were in fact affirmations. Suppose I was having a problem being impatient with Brother George who was living with me in the community. By creating a little prayer like: "Thank you Lord for helping me be patient with Brother George," I would be putting information on my brain which would give a command to change my behavior when I am with Brother George.

In all of our monasteries, there were miles of corridor which we had to walk daily, often in silence. In order to use that time in a constructive way, we were instructed to have these little prayers at our finger tips and to repeat them over and over again as we walked the corridors either on the way to or from the chapel or our cells. By mentally repeating the prayer we were impressing the image of "being patient with George" on our sub-conscious mind; and one morning we would awaken to find that we were indeed "patient with Brother George."

You may not have miles of corridor in your home but you do have quiet time during the day when you can conveniently use affirmations. In your car, for example, is a good place to use affirmations or while waiting in a doctor's office, walking the dog, doing the dishes, or using public transportation. Of course, if you have leisure time at home each morning, afternoon or evening, you may even have the luxury of sitting at a desk or table to write affirmations.

While preparing to write this chapter, I wanted to add several affirmations to my day. I began composing and using them while exercising each day either walking or riding a stationary bike. In order to make the process more convenient, I put the affirmations on cassette tape, repeating each affirmation 10 times. (Ten or twelve affirmations, each repeated 10 times, do not take longer than 10 minutes to recite.) It was then possible to listen to the affirmations in the morning while shaving, brushing my teeth, and exercising. I kept the tape with me in the car and used it during the day and played it at night as I was falling asleep. It doesn't take long to experience results when affirmations are used regularly and often in this way!

One of the affirmations I used was: "I, Justin, have perfectly formed and healthy knees." I chose this affirmation because I recently had an operation on my left knee and was unable to run as a daily exercise. After using the affirmation for only one week, my knee felt so good that I was able to run again.

Affirmations and Education

Affirmations have been a valuable means of behavioral change in education for years. As a child in second grade, I recall being kept in the classroom after school with other students who had been misbehaving. We were told to take out a piece of paper and write one hundred times: "I am a good boy." Of course we didn't understand the process but it worked. As we wrote that statement over and over again, it became impressed on our brains at the subconscious level of mind. Sometimes this process had to be repeated, but it was effective.

Take a moment to consider and clarify for yourself the uniqueness of this affirming approach as opposed to some common misunderstandings of discipline. It doesn't take a great deal of imagination to grasp how much more effective "I am a good boy" will be than having a child stay after class to write one hundred times something like "I will never throw erasers (i.e., disrupt the classroom) again." By the time this sentence has been written 100 times, the fertile imagination of the child will have discovered 100 other things that can be done to 'disrupt the classroom' because that is what is being impressed.

Teachers can use affirmations directed toward students who have many difficulties. For example, if Johnny is having difficulty with math a teacher can repeat over and over to him, whenever he does something correct, "See, you can do it!" or "Johnny, you are getting better at math with each problem you solve." A teacher who will take the time to use affirmations like this can do a great deal to help impress these positive ideas on the brain of the student.

These supportive statements can be used by teachers to help students with positive self-image, athletic skills, behavior issues, as well as academic performance.

Administrators can use affirmations in the same manner with their teachers. Like all human beings, professionals can profit from positive comments made by people in positions of authority. "Mary, the presentation you made in your physics lab today was excellent." "Henry, I really appreciate the way you handled that discipline problem today with Tony Smith."

Teachers can also use positive statements to build one another's self-esteem. "Terri, I really appreciated your taking the time to listen to me this afternoon." "Rose, you were so patient with Sylvia yesterday. I hope I can grow to be that patient myself!"

This kind of affirming can take place in any work environment. I put the emphasis on education because of the effects it can have on youth and on our future history.

Affirmations and Counseling

I know a therapist who has used affirmations with outstanding results. She first helps the client clearly describe the desired effect and then assists in creating an affirmation. The client is then instructed to write the affirmation twenty times each morning, afternoon and evening. The morning and afternoon sessions are strictly writing but the evening session is to be done with writing and speaking. By speaking aloud, the client activates the added senses of speech and hearing as well as physical motion and sight. The more senses that are used in the process the more effective the affirmation can be. This kind of written repetition of affirmations can produce amazing results in any area of life.

The following story (based on an actual life situation) dramatically demonstrates the power of words.

A radio announcer was busy with a talk show on Christmas Eve. It was a bitter cold night with a raging blizzard piling up snow everywhere. One of the callers was a woman who was trapped in her car with two young children and she begged the radio announcer to please send out a tow truck before she and her children froze to death.

After hanging up the phone the announcer wondered why the woman called the radio station instead of a garage but being concerned for her he called a garage, spoke to the owner who was used to these kinds of situations, and gave him directions to the location indicated by the caller.

Because the distance was considerable and the road conditions so bad, the truck driver hesitated but decided to leave immediately thinking that he didn't want to have the woman and children on his conscience.

Later that night the garageman called, informing the radio announcer that he did find the stalled car with its three occupants—and none too soon. The mother and the children were wrapped in blankets and would not have lasted much longer in the sub-zero temperature. He brought them into town and found a warm comfortable place for them to spend the night.

The announcer asked the garageman, "Did you ask why she didn't call a garage?"

"That's another thing," he replied. "When I got there, I was puzzled. The car was stalled where there was no phone anywhere for miles and she had no car phone. I started to ask where she'd phoned from, then got busy with her car and forgot about it."

The next day the announcer tried to find the woman but she and the children had already left.

For several years at Christmas time the announcer got a postal card without a name or address that simply read, "Thank you!"

Some time later the announcer published the story, still puzzled about the phone call. A psychologist who read the story contacted the announcer reporting that he had a client who related the same story—a woman who didn't really understand how the announcer got her message. There was, of course, no phone in or near the car. What she did was talk aloud to the voice coming over the car radio. She cried out over and over again, giving directions to the spot, and about an hour later the tow truck arrived. The psychologist could not explain the facts, he could only report what he knew.

The force of words can indeed be something powerful!!!

Affirmations and Sales

Professional sales people can testify to the importance and power of affirmative statements. Stating the facts over and over again, getting the customer to visualize himself or herself using a product or service and, especially, encouraging the customer to talk as if the product or service were already theirs is a sure way of making a sale.

A friend of mine who teaches programs similar to those I teach, was contacted by mail. A company who produces self-help programs told him of the good things they had heard about his work and invited him (without cost or obligation) to make a trip to a distant city to see their product. My friend was flattered by the letter and was interested in the offer because he had never been to the designated city and looked upon the trip as a mini-vacation.

When he arrived, he joined a large group who had come from all over the country. Together they were familiarized with the programs of the company. Some members of the group had already been involved in selling the programs and began to share their success stories. The entire group was asked to consider their own particular situations and share in their own words how they could imagine selling the programs in their home cities.

After only one day, the company asked for an investment of $15,000 for a set of sample programs that would net the buyer twice that amount after their sale. My friend had no intention at all of making such an investment but, because of the skillful use of language and getting him to verbalize his own life situation, he signed a contract and came home with $15,000 worth of programs. Words, effectively used, are a powerful means of effecting change!

I remember when I was first getting started in the fields of teaching and preaching. After a presentation, a gentleman who eventually came to be a good friend commented that I was a good salesman. It was the first time I had been called by that title and I commented that I didn't understand. He then explained that he saw me as someone who was selling the truth and doing a good job of it.

After reflecting on the entire situation I realized that the description was accurate. It is true—by using carefully chosen words with conviction and helping people imagine their application in life, anyone can have a powerful impact on another. Think of the impact Jesus had on the people of his time—and the generations after him who received his word second hand. Think of the power Ghandi's words had on the nation of India or the power Lao Tzu's tiny volume, *Tao Te Ching*, has had on generations of Chinese.

When you look at life from this point of view, each of us is trying to influence the other. We are all, in a sense, sales people. We find bits and pieces of the truth that work for us and then seek to get others to accept these same truths, believing that "if they have worked for me, they will also work for you." The fact of the matter is, our words can and do influence others in one direction or another. We therefore need to be careful, with ourselves and others, of the words we utter.

Qualities of Effective Affirmations

First Person

There are several qualities of effective affirmations. First of all, affirmations are more effective when created in the *first person*. This is because you have direct and immediate control of yourself—you do not have direct control over others. Including your first name will reinforce your identification. For example, "I, Mary, am always organized in everything I do." In this statement, Mary identifies herself in a very direct and personal way. The subconscious mind is given a powerful directive with this kind of identification.

Present Tense

Another characteristic of effective affirmations is that they are stated in the *present tense*. The mind exists and functions only in the present; therefore statements made in the present tense have an immediate and lasting effect. For example, "I, Mary, am always organized in everything I do." Even though Mary may not be organized at the present time, using the affirmation in this manner will impress the image on the brain. Once it reaches the subconscious level, it will have its effect and create a quality of character that will be present always.

When I was teaching high school one of the girls named Jo had a strong dislike for a classmate. She expressed that dislike frequently by saying: "She makes me sick!" Even in casual conversation if the name of this particular student came up, she would say: "She makes me sick!"

One day I was attending a party at which both of these girls were present. At one point, Jo approached the refreshment table, poured herself a glass of punch and turned to return to her seat. It happened that the other was girl was standing directly behind her at the table so when Jo turned around they met face to face. As soon as she recognized the person behind her Jo immediately became sick to her stomach and hurried off to the rest room where she promptly "tossed her cookies."

She had repeated the statement so many times with so much emotion that when she confronted the person the subconscious (which took the statement literally) gave the command to her body to become sick.

What you state in the present tense becomes a part of the reality present to the mind. The results follow just as surely as night follows day!

Positive Terms

Affirmations are more effective if they use only *positive terms*. A person wishing to stop smoking, for example, would do better to speak in terms of healthy lungs rather than in terms of "stopping smoking." An affirmation stating: "I, John, have clean and healthy lungs," will cause the brain to send the body whatever messages are necessary to create that reality. Creating "clean and healthy lungs" will demand that the body throw off a habit like smoking.

A long time ago I was examining an ejector razor. The instrument was designed to hold a shaving blade very tightly. If you tried to simply remove the blade, you could spend an enormous amount of time and never be successful. However, if you took a package of new blades and simply aligned the new blade next to the old one and concentrated on putting the new blade in, the old one automatically slipped out the other end of the razor.

That condition is similar to the way the mind works. If you become completely preoccupied with a positive thought, the negative ones automatically get pushed out of consciousness and lose their effectiveness.

Suppose you bite your nails and you want to stop the habit. An affirmation like: "I, Justin, have no desire to bite my nails" forces the mind to picture "biting nails" in order to understand the statement. As a result, "biting nails" is being reinforced in the mind. It is much better for you to create an affirmation like this: "I, Justin, have perfectly shaped nails of average length." This kind of an affirmation forces your mind to create an image of the final result. As it is impressed over and over again by using the affirmation, the mind directs the body to do what is necessary to allow the nails to grow to average length.

Specific

One of the more challenging aspects of forming an affirmation is being *specific*. The more accurate and detailed the affirmation, the more effective it will be. Suppose, for example, you are interested in improving your health. Using the affirmation, "I, Justin, am in perfect health," is a good affirmation. But if you determine what is specifically going to create health for you, the affirmation can have more power. You may determine that you need to add exercise to your daily routine in order to be more healthy. An appropriate affirmation might then be: "I, (your name), walk briskly for one-half hour after supper every Monday, Wednesday and Friday." This kind of affirmation gives specific direction to the brain and will have a greater effect.

Short

A good affirmation is *short*. A single declarative statement is far better than a whole paragraph. Such short statements can be put on a card and placed on the bathroom mirror, in a wallet or purse, attached to the dashboard of your automobile, to the refrigerator door or placed on your desk where they will be easily seen. It is a simple matter to commit short statements to memory so they can be repeated frequently during the day.

You may be interested in correcting some malfunctions in your body such as deformed toe nails or feet, painful knees or shoulders, poorly functioning eyes or skin problems. Instead of writing one long affirmation for all of these problems it would be more effective to create several affirmations like the following:

I, (your name), have perfectly formed and healthy toe nails.
I, _____, have perfectly formed and healthy feet.
I, _____, have perfectly formed and healthy knees.
I, _____, have perfectly formed and healthy shoulders.
I, _____, have perfectly formed and healthy eyes.
I, _____, have perfectly formed and healthy skin.

Written

Confirming affirmations with the *written* word will not only help you be more exact, but the very fact of writing them is activating another sense that will help impress the information more effectively on the brain.

By committing the affirmation to writing you can carefully choose words and repeat the same sequence over and over again. Such written affirmations can become effective for an entire group of people. A football team, for example, which uses a chant like "We're number one!" can have this message more powerfully impressed on their brains by having the statement printed on posters in the stadium as well as chanted by the entire crowd.

The same effect can be achieved by a slogan adopted by members of a company, printed on their individual calling cards, and placed on bulletin boards.

With Feeling

Finally, affirmations will be most effective if they are used with *emotion* and *enthusiasm*. Consciously putting accents on important words and using physical gestures, even when the statements are repeated mentally can have a greater impact on brain cells. Repeating the affirmations out loud (and, when appropriate, with others) generates an internal excitement that makes a deeper impression. As with writing, the very fact of speaking out loud activates another sense that will help impress the information more effectively on the brain.

This very process was used in the United States during World War II to get the general population behind the war effort. It got people to buy war bonds; it got them up in the morning to go to work at jobs many had never imagined themselves doing. Hitler used affirmations and taught the entire populace to chant with enthusiasm. Although this particular cause was entirely negative, the effects were powerful enough to activate millions of people.

A negative example here is as important as a positive one. As you become aware of the power of affirmations, rather than becoming anxious it is more helpful to become attentive. What you choose to put in your mind or allow into your mind will be impressed on your brain and will shape your action accordingly. The impact on the thought process is enormous and the effects are powerful. The same dramatic results can be achieved regardless of the thrust of the affirmations.

Famous "affirmations" that have been recited over and over with enthusiasm and emotion for the general public include such phrases as "Breakfast of Champions," "99 and 44/100% Pure," "When you care enough to send the very best," and many more. Repetition of these statements has a strong effect on the minds of individuals who hear them, so much effect that we buy the products.

Qualities of Effective Affirmations

1. First person (using your own name)
2. Present tense
3. Positive terms
4. Specific
5. Short
6. Written
7. Used with emotion

Sample Affirmations

It is most powerful to create your own affirmations using the guidelines listed; however, models can help you get started. These examples, because they were created for a general audience, will not be as specific as those you tailor-make; but they will be of some value as samples.

Family

I, (your name), daily express my love for each member of my family.

I, _____, daily enjoy quality time with my family.

I, _____, daily and consciously reflect on the good qualities of each member of my family.

Finance

I, _____, am able to generate easily an annual income of $_____.

I, _____, am in complete control of my financial situation.

I, _____, enjoy sharing my abundance with others.

Faith

I, _____, have unlimited potential.

I, _____, believe in the unlimited potential of others.

I, _____, meditate daily in the morning and in the evening.

Friends

I, _____, choose positive thinking and loving people as friends.

I, _____, take time to cultivate deep friendships.

I, _____, enjoy giving my time to others when they are in need.

Fitness

I, _____, am able to easily maintain my ideal weight of _____ lbs.

I, _____, enjoy a regular regimen of daily exercise.

I, _____, enjoy sufficient and restful sleep every night.

Formal or Informal Education

I, _____, take time daily to fill my mind with positive and healthy thoughts.

I, _____, choose entertainment that is good for me.

I, _____, attend at least one week-end seminar or workshop annually.

Fun

I, _____, take time daily to have fun.

I, _____, laugh easily, heartily and often.

I, _____, enjoy and share jokes daily.

Suggested Activities

1. Begin with a single affirmation.
   a. Describe some positive change you would like to make in your life.
   b. Using the seven guidelines in this chapter, compose an affirmation, that states the change as present reality.
   c. Write the affirmation 20 times in the morning, 20 times after lunch, and 20 times before going to sleep. At least once during the day speak the affirmation aloud each time you write it.
   d. After doing this for one month, note the changes that have taken place.

2. Using several affirmations:
   a. Make a list of affirmations you wish to use.
   b. Put each affirmation on a single card.
   c. Place the cards in places where you can see them during the day:
      • on the mirror in your bathroom
      • on the refrigerator
      • in your purse or wallet
      • on the dashboard of the car
      • in a prominent place on your desk
      • in the book you are reading
      • on the TV, etc.
   d. Every time you see an affirmation, repeat it several times.
   e. Use affirmations this way for a month, making notes on the changes that occur.

3. Using a tape recorder:
   a. Make a list of affirmations.
   b. Put the affirmations on tape—repeating each one 10 times.
   c. Play the tape:
      • in the morning as you are preparing for the day.
      • in the car.
      • at night as you are falling asleep.
   d. Use this procedure for a month and note the results.

4. Experiment with other creative ways for using affirmations.
   You can devise several combinations of the approaches. If you choose to become a student of your own process, it will be helpful to have notes on the approach you used. You may discover that particular approaches work better for specific kinds of positive change. If you keep notes on affirmations you plan to focus on next, you may find some of them disappear from your list because they are accomplished while you are working on others.

5

ATTITUDES

The word attitude refers to a point of view or an intellectual or psychological position. In space technology, for example, we talk about the attitude of a spacecraft, a description of its position or how it is being viewed in space.

When speaking about attitude in daily life we are talking about the way a person perceives the world and/or life situations. This particular aspect of life is important since it determines to a great degree the experience of the individual who is doing the viewing. As you begin a new week for example, you can look at Monday as being a beginning of new opportunity or you can view it as "Blue Monday." Your perspective has everything to do with the kind of experience you have.

In this chapter we will examine first of all, attitudes toward self, then attitudes toward others and finally attitudes toward all life experience.

Attitudes toward Self

Attitudes toward self are perhaps the most important and most fundamental attitudes of all. How you view yourself, more often than not, determines how you view others and the world in which you live. It is advantageous, therefore, to develop and maintain a positive mental attitude toward yourself.

Your attitude regarding self is a result of the sum total of all the thoughts that you have gathered about yourself from the time you were born to the present moment. If that information is predominantly positive, you will feel good about yourself. If the information that you have gathered about yourself over the years is predominantly negative, you will feel badly about yourself.

It is true that others help you build your self-image. Parents and teachers, for example, have a powerful impact as you grow. If they constantly help you know and use your assets, you more easily build a positive image. If they help you concentrate on your shortcomings, you can develop a more negative attitude. Regardless of what others have given you or how you see yourself now, you can change your perception if you so choose.

Here are a few suggestions on how to see yourself in a more positive light.

Learn to Say "Thank You"

There are a great many ways that all of us can build a more healthy self-image. For example, when you are given an honest or deserved compliment, it is important that you learn how to stand on your own two feet with your head held high and accept the compliment by simply saying, "Thank You." Accepting honest compliments graciously is an important way of boosting your own self-image.

I have frequently seen individuals given honest compliments, but because they had a poor self-image, could not say "Thank You" easily. One day a student of mine came into class wearing a beautiful sweater. It looked unique, so I asked if she had made it herself. She replied in the affirmative and I complemented her. Her immediate response was, "Thank you. But you know, Father, I dropped a stitch in the back." With that, she pulled the back part of the sweater forward to point out where there was a flaw in the stitching. I would never have been able to detect that flaw, but even if I had, my comment on her skill was still valid. If her self-image had been healthy, she could simply have said, "Thank you" even though she knew the final product was not perfect.

Share Your Successes

Another way in which you can build self-image is to get into the habit of sharing your successes. As part of the follow up to the "Success:Full Living" classes we encourage graduates at reunions to begin meetings by telling their success stories. Verbalizing successes of any kind is a way of reaffirming your abilities and strengthening them.

A good way of forcing yourself to look at your successes is to create a scrapbook. I remember when a cousin of mine was competing in the Miss America Pageant. She won at the local level, but the college she was attending did not approve of the pageant and issued an ultimatum stating that she would either have to give up her title of "Miss Omaha" or be expelled from school. After a great deal of consideration, she made the decision to complete her education. This decision resulted in international publicity and soon she began to receive letters of support and congratulations from individuals all over the world. She saved all these letters and newspaper articles, and every time she opens that book and shares it with someone, she is able to reaffirm herself, the choice she made, the person she is.

I frequently get questioned by students as to whether sharing successes is a form of bragging. My response to that question has always been, "It depends on how you handle the situation." Bragging implies an attitude of superiority and the braggart mentally holds himself or herself above others, looking downward psychologically. When you are honestly sharing successes and your attitude is one of equality with the person to whom you are speaking, the situation becomes an invitation for the other person to share success stories also. In this case, not only the speaker but the listener can be assisted in helping to build a more positive self-image.

Use Meditation to Improve Self-Image

As previously stated, the way you see yourself at present is the result of all the thoughts you have gathered about yourself over the years. You can, however, improve that image by filling your mind with more positive thoughts about yourself.

More often than not, excessive drinking, smoking and eating are symptoms of poor self-image. In many of these cases creating a more positive self-image can dispel the symptoms and produce more satisfying behavior.

By going into meditation and repeating an affirmation like: "I am lovable and capable," anyone can impress a more positive image on their sub-conscious. A significant and permanent change of attitude toward self will alter self-destructive behavior.

I remember a middle-aged gentleman who came to one of my workshops with the express purpose of losing weight. After learning the mechanics of meditation he began a visualization and affirmation combination. In a totally relaxed state, he daily pictured himself stepping on a scale and saw the indicator pointing to his ideal weight. At the same time he pictured a calendar on the wall and an "X" drawn through the date he wanted to reach his goal (allowing a 6 week period for a 25 lb. weight loss). To this visualization he added the affirmation: "I, Pete, burn up excess fat and carbohydrates so that by June 25, I weigh 150 lbs."

During the following weeks, he began to lose weight and he did not change any of his eating habits. He did, however, add exercise to his daily schedule and when the date of his accomplishment arrived he had reached his goal.

Sometimes our mental perceptions of self are far from the objective reality but the image does have its effect.

Maxwell Maltz in his book *Psycho-Cybernetics* describes a person who came to him with what she called a facial disfigurement. For years she had perceived her nose as extremely large and as an affliction. Of course her personality had a corresponding disorder.

Upon careful examination, Dr. Maltz concluded that her nose was normal and proved it to her by taking her picture and comparing it with other pictures he had of people with "normal" noses. The woman left the office intellectually convinced but she still felt uncomfortable in public.

Every day, as she looked into the mirror, she began to see her nose in a different way. Twenty-one days later the personality disorder disappeared and she lived happily ever after (that is, in regard to her nose!).

The point is: perceive yourself as limited and you will develop limiting behavior. Perceive yourself as unlimited and you will develop unlimiting behavior.

Meditation is the most powerful tool for putting new information on the brain. Develop skill in this technique and you can tap into your unlimited potential.

Attitudes toward Others

I began this chapter with self-image because I believe all human beings understand the loving process by starting with self. Only after children have learned to love themselves are they able to understand their connection with others and capable of building meaningful and loving relationships with others. Building successful, mature and lasting relationships with others is one of the bases for understanding and growing in love with the Divine. A positive self-image is therefore fundamental to all love relationships.

Once you have the experience of building self-image, it is much easier to understand that struggle in others.

Not long ago, I met a young man who was very critical of his alcoholic father. He was habitually angry with his dad, constantly making demands, offering solutions and creating confrontations. In order to deal with his anxiety, the son began to drink and discovered his own alcoholism. When he had to deal with the problem himself, he became much more understanding of his father. Working on the problem himself made it possible for him to find effective ways of working with his father.

Consider your own person. You have one side that is actualized and another part of you that can still be explored and developed. (Some people out of the need to make a sharper distinction, or not as careful as they might be about negative images, refer to these dynamics as a good side and a bad side or a light side and dark side.) This situation is common to all human beings. If you prefer to have others look for and concentrate on your strengths and overlook your weaknesses, surely you can understand that others would prefer the same.

Think back to a time when you made a mistake. Recall the feeling of embarrassment. At a time like that you know the last thing in the world you need is someone standing over you and saying: "You fell on your face, you dummy!"

On the other hand, recall a time when you made a mistake and someone was there to understand and offer a helping hand. Someone who is able to comfort you by saying: "It's all right, we all make mistakes. Let me help!"

It has been interesting for me over the years to watch young people who are in "LUV." When two people are infatuated with each other, their viewpoint is totally positive. They can see only goodness in each other and, as a result, experience love. They have their minds totally closed to viewing any imperfection in each other, and it becomes impossible to talk to them about potential problems in the relationship. If you mention something negative about their partner, you may hear them say, "Not my honey!"

As the years go on, their viewpoint begins to change and they have a tendency to focus more and more on shortcomings and faults. It can happen, over a period of years, that attitudes can shift 180 degrees. When that happens and they begin viewing only the weaknesses in each other, they will also begin to fall out of love.

As a marriage counselor I frequently had to deal with situations like this. The wife usually was on the phone first, asking for an appointment. She would arrive at my office and I would say, "I understand that you have a problem," and she would answer, "Yes!" I would ask if it was serious and she would answer, "Indeed it is!" My next question would be, "What is the problem?" and she would immediately respond, "My husband!" At that point, I would listen to a long litany of all the terrible things that this man is and does. When she finished singing her litany, I hated him! Why? I would never have met the man, but all I knew was the negative side of his person. At that point, I would find myself thinking, "I never want to meet *this* man in a dark alley!"

As you might expect, when I would call the husband into the office he would sing the same litany about his wife.

In cases like this a simple technique would work like magic. I would tell the couple to each get a little notebook and every night before they went to sleep they were to write at least three good things they found out about their spouse that day—a personality trait, some kind of achievement, or some skill. They were not allowed to share this information, but they had to write down at least three items each night. (They could write more if they wished.) After working on this project for a week, they would come back to my office. The wife would share in detail all the information that she had gathered about her husband; he would have to sit quietly and listen. Then the husband would share all the good things he learned about his wife that week and she had to listen. After only one of these sessions, both parties would leave my office feeling better about each other. The relationship would begin to change and heal.

The only action taken was directing their attention to the good present in the other. Once that happened, their attitudes began to change immediately.

This technique can be used in dealing with anyone. I remember living in a rather large community years ago and having a difficult time with one of the friars in the community. One night I sat down in my room and thought I would write down all the good things I knew about this person in order to develop a more positive attitude. With pen in hand, I thought and thought and thought. I could find nothing good to write about him. So, I started a little project. I carried a notebook around with me and every time I saw him do anything that was positive, I wrote it down. If I saw him smile, I made a note. If I saw him open a door for someone, I would write it down. Any positive comments that I heard from others I noted. In the evening, in the privacy of my room, I started to make a list. (I got a very long list in a very short time.) What happened then was truly a revelation; perhaps one of the most important lessons I ever learned in my life. After a period of about six weeks I realized that we had become friends and he hadn't changed at all! He didn't know about my personal project and so continued to be his normal, natural self. It was I who changed. When that happened, the relationship also changed.

Attitudes toward Life Situations

In the same way that you can change your attitude toward self or toward others, you can also change your attitude toward any life situation. Let me use the example of death.

Many people in our society believe that death is the ultimate tragedy when, in fact, death is a very important part of life. If you have fear or anxiety regarding death, it is only because you view it from a negative perspective. Change your viewpoint and your relationship and experience with death will change also.

There has been a great deal written about this subject in recent years. One of the first volumes to help the general public understand the positive aspects of death was a book titled *Life After Life* by Raymond Moody. In this volume, the author relates the experiences of people who have gone through a death experience and survived. These are people from different faiths, people who had no religious conviction and people from different cultural backgrounds. Essentially, their experiences were the same.

At the moment of death, they experienced their astral body (the perfect energy form of the physical body) leave their physical body and float above the scene. From that vantage point they were able to see the people who were working on their body when, for example, they were in a hospital. In that suspended position, they describe the magnificence of the experience as being "totally immersed in love." Others spoke of it as being "the most beautiful experience" they had ever had. Some described how they would think of a loved one and immediately find themselves present with that loved one.

They then perceived a light, and when they started moving toward it, they found themselves going through a tunnel of light at great speed. At the end of the tunnel, they saw either a figure of Christ or a light form which they knew to be Divine Presence. They also experienced the presence of loved ones who had already died and were there to greet them. At some point they experienced a door, a gate, or a bridge and knew that if they moved in that direction they would not be able to come back. They were then either asked to return or were told to return because they had unfinished business. They found themselves moving back again through the tunnel of light eventually hovering, once again, over their own body. As they descended to reenter the body, they began again to feel physical sensations.

All of these experiences have been described as positive! In fact, the majority of people who have had these experiences lost their fear of death because now they knew it to be truly wonderful. If only all of us could develop this attitude!

It has been difficult for me, as a priest, to walk into situations where the attitude toward death is negative and depressing. In a memorable case, I went into a hospital room and explained to the patient that I was there to help in the healing process and asked if he believed healing was possible. He confided to me that he was dying and asked me to pray with him. When we finished, he asked me not to tell his family that he was dying because he did not want them to worry.

Leaving the room to meet the family in the corridor, I found everyone distraught, some in tears. The daughter informed me that they had just gotten word from the doctor that their father was dying, but she immediately added, "Please, Father, don't tell him. We don't want him to worry."

In a situation like this, individuals who love each other very much choose to ignore a very important experience that, if shared, could bring them much closer together. They choose to talk about the weather and other mundane topics and throw away a perfect opportunity for deepening their love and sharing their lives.

Because of my family background, I had a healthy attitude toward death from my earliest childhood. Death was experienced as part of life. Bodies were waked in private homes and everyone in the neighborhood came to visit. The kitchen, of course, was always a busy place and either the basement or the garage became the bar. As people gathered to share the death experience they also celebrated life together.

As I grew older and picked up present day American culture, my attitudes became negative. I had to consciously rebuild a positive attitude. I began to pay attention to the example of special people who saw death from a life-perspective.

One such learning experience began when I was living abroad. I had completed a four month stay in Israel and had just finished packing to move to Italy when I got a call from the United States. A close friend informed me that a mutual friend of ours, and an employee of his, had just lost his 5-year-old daughter to leukemia. He asked if it were possible for me to come back for the funeral since it would help the parents a great deal. He could forward the necessary funds for the ticket if I could make the trip. I told him I had just finished packing and could be on my way in only a few hours.

When I arrived, he met me at the airport and asked if we could immediately visit with the parents. I was eager to see both of them, so we met at a restaurant where the parents related how, over the last few years, they had been caring for their daughter. They had taken the child to Mexico to become involved in a Laetrile program. They flew to Europe for another kind of treatment and eventually ended up in a west coast hospital where the child went into a coma. While sitting quietly in the hospital room the father had a very important insight. He told his wife, "Honey, if God gave us Susan to teach us a lesson and we've already learned the lesson, perhaps it's time for her to go home." After a bit of consideration the wife agreed, and the two of them knelt down beside the child's bed. They spoke aloud, even though there was no visible response, letting the child know that they understood, and if she felt it was time for her to leave this life plane it was perfectly all right with them. Both parents saw the body of their child relax at that moment and a half hour later she slept peacefully away in death.

At the wake these parents were consoling everyone and saying things like, "Don't worry, Susan is in Heaven," or "It's O.K., we've successfully raised one of our children." Although these people experienced a great deal of grief in having to separate with their child, they taught me and many other people about the positive aspects of death.

In trying to help others create a more positive image of death, I have often described death in terms of a trip. Imagine yourself standing on a pier in New York when a cruise ship is about to depart. The ship is filled with excited people. The band is playing, there are people throwing streamers, others are eating, drinking and singing, all eagerly awaiting the departure of the ship. You see your loved ones on board this ship and you are really happy for them, excited about the opportunity they have to make this wonderful trip. As the ship pulls away you experience the separation, but deep down inside you say to yourself, "Someday I'll be able to make that trip!"

I think this image is an appropriate one for death. If you can perceive the person who has died as the one who has chosen to make this exciting journey to love and peace it will be a lot easier for you to deal with the separation and be at peace in terms of where the other person is.

Gibran in his poem on death wrote: "What is it to die but to free the breath from its restless ties that it may rise and expand, and seek God unencumbered?"*

Any other life experience that may be painful or difficult can also be viewed from a positive perspective and then be dealt with in a meaningful way. As I have said before, I believe that all life experience is good. All of it! Some may be pleasant and some unpleasant, but it is all good. How you view it makes the difference.

Suppose you and a friend both receive a notice in the mail that you have won a free trip to Italy. You view the situation in all of its positive aspects. You picture being at an Italian sidewalk cafe, enjoying a drink in the early evening. You visualize yourself experiencing the beauty and magnificence of the cathedrals. You imagine yourself with artists in Florence and so on. As a result, you get very excited about the trip and look forward to it with eager expectation.

Your friend, on the other hand, views the situation in a completely different way. Your friend begins to think: "This will be the first time I am flying over the ocean. What if the plane goes down; I can't swim!" "How am I going to communicate with other people; I don't know Italian?" "I have been told the water is not good; maybe I'll get sick." The same experience is

---

The Prophet, by Kahlil Gibran, published by Alfred A. Knopf, 1962. Renewal of copyright © 1951 by Administrators C.T.A. of Kahlil Gibran Estate and Mary G. Gibran.

approached with fear and apprehension. The experience is different only because the thought process is different.

Conclusion

Life is too short to waste thinking of possible negative aspects. You can experience your life as valuable and thrilling by simply getting in the habit of thinking of yourself, others and life situations in a positive way. Begin a new chapter in your life by working through some of the suggested activities that follow. By directing your thoughts more positively, your life will become a more positive experience.

SUGGESTED ACTIVITIES

1. Since we all must begin with ourselves, every evening for one week write down your own accomplishments of the day. (Be careful not to leave things off your list just because they weren't planned or because they seem too ordinary. Consider how many people didn't get their shoes polished/car washed/shopping done today.) At the end of the week, read the whole list. Notice the affect it has on your attitude about yourself.

2. Keep a scrap book or journal of your own day-to-day accomplishments. Look through it frequently, even more often if you feel down.

3. For one week, share daily with at least one other person something positive about yourself, some success you have achieved or something good that is happening to you.

4. Choose one person in your life and share only good things about them for one day. Notice how readily positive feelings arise.

5. If you find you are struggling with a relationship to someone at work or home, someone toward whom you feel resentment or anger, at the end of each day write down three positive characteristics, personality traits or accomplishments you know about the person. After one week notice the changes in your attitude toward this person.
   • If you combine these last two exercises, you can sometimes begin a very effective *Good Rumor Campaign*. It is amazing to watch the many ways in which a broad spectrum of often automatic attitudes can change as a result of this kind of interference.

6. Allow a situation in your life that you have considered difficult or painful to come to mind. Spend time thinking of the opportunities and advantages attached to it. Put your results on paper and look at them regularly.

6

GOALS

Your life is a sizable package. It might, at times, seem to be almost impossible to maneuver. However, if you have a way to "divide and conquer," as well as a few organizational tools, taking control of your life can be a simple matter.

Divide and Conquer

Years ago when I first began teaching, our department acquired a large electronic organ with a full pedal-board. We frequently had to move this instrument to other parts of the building. The weight, of course, was impossible for a single person to handle. The company from whom we bought the organ suggested that we also purchase what they called a piano truck. It consisted of only two small dollies and a strong belt about four inches wide. With the help of one other person, the pedal board, could be removed; then by lifting one end of the instrument sufficiently to push the lip of the first dolly under one side and slipping the second dolly under the opposite side, we could strap the two dollies to the console by wrapping the belt securely around them and the organ. A lever attached to each dolly could then be easily lifted, putting the organ on wheels. After that, one person could roll the organ anywhere in the school.

This chapter is designed to help you "move" your life. By mentally taking it apart and using the tools it offers, you will be able to take control of and give direction to your life. A task that you may have seen before as difficult or impossible can become simple, exciting and effective.

Individuals frequently work on their lives in the same way politicians deal with government, i.e., they work essentially on the immediate crisis, then move to the next crisis. This method of dealing with life is not really efficient and can be very frustrating, not to mention exhausting.

A better approach is goal setting and planning. Let's use the image of a garden. You can grow anything you wish in a garden, provided you do what is necessary.

When I joined the Order, most of our houses had gardens attached to them. As recently as ten years ago when I was working at a retreat center on the north side of Indianapolis our friars had a small patch of ground which was used each year for a garden. As soon as the crocus would break through the ground, the friars got busy preparing the soil. One would dig up the ground, another would bring in manure, still others were out getting plants and seeds. There was always a great deal of garden enthusiasm as spring came upon us. With all this interest it didn't take long for the plot of ground to materialize into a beautiful garden with carefully delineated rows. Around the whole garden we built a fence protecting the plot. However as spring wore into summer, enthusiasm for the garden frequently waned.

One year I had to leave the center for a speaking engagement and was gone for nearly three weeks. On my return I decided for a change of pace to get out into the garden to weed, but I couldn't find the garden. It was completely buried in weeds! My first thought was to get to the largest weeds, some of which were three or four feet high. I walked carefully through the garden, pulling out one weed at a time and soon had a large pile. After working for an hour or so I stepped back to look at the garden and it was still a mess! Disposing of the weeds that had been collected, I threw up my hands in despair and walked away.

The next day, again having the urge to go to the garden, I decided to use a different approach. Getting down on my hands and knees at the beginning of the first row, I decided to pull out all the weeds in that one row, carefully exposing each plant. After about an hour, I was able to step back and see one full row completely clean with the plants clearly visible. Although only a short amount of time had passed, I could see progress. As I got rid of the piles of weeds, I felt so good about what had been accomplished, I decided to come back the next day and work on the second row.

Working on your life can be a similar kind of process. If you try to work on the entire thing all at once, doing a little bit here and a little bit there, you may step back to get an overview and see little progress, in which case you are liable to lose your interest. However, if you can divide your life into workable units and concentrate on one at a time, it is possible to start making noticeable change so that when you step back you can see the progress. You will then be motivated to continue and do more.

A simple method of breaking down your life is to work with categories. I have devised seven categories. You have already seen them in the chapter on affirmations. They are only suggestions and can be added to or subtracted from. What is important is that you understand the process.

The seven categories are:
- Faith • Family • Finance (Work) • Fitness (Health)
- Friends (Social Life) • Formal/Informal Education
- Fun

Balance

My first point regarding these categories is that each is of equal importance. None takes precedence over another. In other words, I believe we all need to have goals in each one of these areas. Making one category more important than the rest will create a lopsided human being.

Most often when you or I are told that another person has become successful, that description implies financial success. I certainly have no objection to people being successful financially, but if that is their only area of interest they can very easily become successful financiers and unbalanced human beings.

Some years ago, when I was teaching music, I attended a National Music Education Association Convention in Philadelphia and stayed at a Hilton Hotel. While there, I found in one of the drawers an interesting book titled *Be My Guest* by Conrad Hilton.

As a small child, Conrad Hilton was found one day by his friends sitting on a curb opposite the only hotel in the little town where he was raised. His hands were cupped under his chin, his elbows were on his knees and he was staring at the hotel across the street. The youngsters came upon him and asked, "Connie, what are you doin'?" He replied simply, "Someday I'm going to own that hotel."

At that young age, he had a clear idea of what he wanted to do with his life. As he grew older and needed a job he went, of course, to the hotel, starting at the very bottom, and began to learn all he could about the hotel business. He eventually became the manager of the hotel and later bought it. The secret to his success was very simple: He said his mother, who was Catholic, taught him how to pray; his father, who was Protestant, taught him how to work; and God gave him the ability to dream.

As the years went on, he became more and more involved in the hotel business. He married, but the business had top priority in his life. As a result the relationships in his family suffered and his wife eventually demanded a divorce in order to stabilize the lives of the children. At this point, a great deal of pain and suffering entered his life because of the imbalance.

As a youngster Conrad Hilton had gone to church daily, but when he decided to remarry it became impossible for him to continue his active participation in the Catholic church. At that point still more pain entered his life.

The lesson here is that if we keep a balance in goal setting in all areas of life, we can achieve in each of them and bring joy and satisfaction into our lives.

Imbalance can happen in any area of life. Take, for example, the area of fitness. I have carried a YMCA membership for years because I exercise daily and their facilities are conveniently located. In most of these facilities, it is common to find young men and women who are involved in bodybuilding. They stand in front of a mirror, flexing their muscles and making it evident how successful they are in this particular area of life. But if their lives revolve only around this activity, they become unbalanced. Ask such a person, for example, to go out to lunch on Tuesday and you might get the response, "Toosday, what day is Toosday?" "You know, Joe, the day you do shoulders." "Oh yeah, shoulders!" Try to carry on a conversation on topics other than bodybuilding techniques or diet and there may be little or no response.

Imbalance can take place in the area of faith. I once met a young man who wanted to spend his entire life praying. In itself that is a good goal. However, in this particular case, the young man spent so much time involved with the church that he was unable to function as a father and husband. He spent a lot of time reading the scriptures and praying, but he was lazy, authoritarian, demanding, impatient and almost impossible to live with. He may have spent a great deal of time praying, but a saint he was not! To be a successful human being you must have balanced goals in each of multiple areas.

Long and Short Range Goals

When discussing goals, it is valuable to talk in terms of long-range and short-range goals. By a long-range goal, I mean one that is at least a year into the future. Short-term goals are ones that are dealt with on a day-to-day basis. A college degree, for example, could be a long-range goal and the classes that must be attended daily, as well as the homework to be accomplished, are the short-range goals.

A young couple about to be engaged may determine that their long-range goal is to be in their own home in five years time with two of their own children. The first short-range goal is the engagement, the next is the wedding. After that they have to work to create a down payment on a home and determine when they want to have their first child.

A high school student of mine determined that he wanted to create an international business by the time he was 30 years old. He then planned an undergraduate as well as a graduate program. While in college he got involved in real estate so that by the time he graduated from the university he had a successful business going. He gathered others who were interested in being a part of the same dream and before the age of 30 he had an international business.

The farther into the future you can set a goal, the easier it is to give your life direction. The future goal becomes the point of reference for everything you do on a day-to-day basis. All of your involvements can be related to this future goal. Choices become simple; all you need to ask is whether the present activity will take you toward the goal or not.

At an educational convention, I once heard a distinguished lecturer say that "human beings do not mature until they make a life commitment" (which of course is a long-range goal). Perhaps you may want to determine if you agree with that statement and examine your life for long-range goals. Short-range goals then are the things we all have to get involved in on a daily basis. Think about your own present commitments and how those commitments help you determine what your daily schedule will be. At the beginning of an average day you usually have a fair idea of some things you want to accomplish. These daily activities, because they relate to the future, put meaning into your life.

Several Goals: One at a Time

Goal setting may sound rather complex, but in daily life it is really simple. You can only work on one goal at a time, but in the course of a day you can work on goals in all seven life areas. In my own life, for example, as soon as I get up in the morning, I get involved in 10-15 minutes of exercise, also repeating positive affirmations during that time. These two activities are goals that fit into the areas of physical and mental fitness. After that, showering, shaving, brushing my teeth and getting ready for the day's work are also activities in the category of fitness. My next activity is meditation (a goal related to "faith"). I then sit at my desk to write and work on correspondence (goals that relate to work and income, which for me is the area of "finance"). On leaving my apartment for morning Mass at The Hermitage, I am joined by members of The Hermitage staff (this activity relates to "faith," as well as to my spiritual "family"). After that, breakfast (relating to "fitness" and to "friends" or social life). Later in the morning, I get involved with "formal or informal education" by reading or studying material for future classes and/or lectures.

Sometimes, long-range goals may not be clear but they are present. In this case you can look into the activities of your day and ask: "What direction is this activity taking me?" "What will be the consequences of this act for the future?" Answering these kinds of questions will help you discover the sub-conscious goals you have.

A person may come home from work every day to relax with a drink or two. As time goes on the individual may be drinking more and more. A logical look at the future will indicate that if this process continues, the goal of "becoming drunk" every evening may follow. The individual may want to reconsider the consequences of this goal.

On a day-to-day basis, we all pick and choose the activities with which we want to become involved. It is important to note that each of these will relate specifically to a goal, either short or long-range.

Note also that the variety indicated by the seven major areas of life is important. It offers a spice to life that creates interest and excitement. Sometimes movement toward a goal may be slow, but as long as there is movement you are successful!

Qualities of Effective Goals

In order for goal setting to be effective, it is useful to consider the following qualities: specific, challenging, written and within a given time frame.

Specific

Perhaps the most important characteristic of goal setting is being *specific*. If I were to ask, "Are you interested in being healthy?" I am sure you would reply in the affirmative. However, "being healthy" is not a goal; it is only a general direction. That kind of statement is too general to be identified as a goal.

On the other hand, suppose you know that you need exercise in your weekly schedule in order to improve your health. You might then set a goal that states, "On Monday, Wednesday and Friday, immediately after supper I will walk for one half hour." That kind of a statement is so specific that at the end of each week you can identify clearly if the goal has been achieved or not.

Challenging

Goals must also be *challenging*. By that I mean, they need to help you stretch. An infant is a wonderful example. Immediately after birth, all babies get involved in kicking and stretching and crying. As they grow, they get involved in more specific kinds of activity. At first it may be something as simple as rolling over, but that is a real challenge for an infant. As they mature, they challenge themselves by crawling, holding themselves upright and eventually getting into the very sophisticated activity of walking.

One of the dangers in American society today is frequent encouragement to "take it easy," or "be comfortable." Balancing work and recreation is essential, but we also need to constantly be reaching for whatever will help up to grow and become better human beings. Grocery shopping may not be an exceptionally difficult activity for some people, however, for a handicapped person getting the shopping done each week may be very challenging. Achieving average grades for one student may be an easy matter, for another achieving an average grade may be a Herculian task. One person may find it very challenging to make friends and to develop social skills, to another those skills may come naturally. What I am suggesting is that you reach out for goals that will make you stretch.

Written

Writing down your goals is not only valuable but sometimes essential. The *written* word helps anyone to be more precise; it also offers a record that will not change.

I learned this important lesson just one year before I was ordained to the priesthood. At that time, a young professor had just returned from Spain to teach moral theology. One day during class he commented that all of us had high ideals of the Franciscan priesthood and that we would do well to preserve those ideals in writing. He suggested that we take time to write an extended essay describing exactly what our ideal of the Franciscan priesthood was. He further suggested that we look to some of the friars we knew and admired and incorporate their characteristics into the essay. At the same time, he suggested that we look at some of the friars that we did not want to emulate and describe their characteristics as ones we did not want to develop.

I thought this suggestion was rather interesting and spent several weeks writing an essay in which I described the kind of Franciscan priest I would like to be. When it was completed I filed it away. Two years later, after I had been in the active ministry for a full year and was preparing to leave on an annual retreat, I remembered the essay and threw it into my suitcase. When I arrived at the retreat center and picked up the essay, I was shocked. In only one year of active ministry, I had gone off on a tangent, moving further and further away from the ideal I had on paper. Because my ideas were carefully preserved in writing, I was able to correct my direction and get myself back to the ideals that were really important for me. That essay may have saved my vocation!

Had I not preserved my ideal in writing it would have been difficult for me to be objective. If one of my confreres, for example, had approached me during that retreat to tell me I was moving away from my earlier ideals, I would have denied the fact. I was very involved in my work and could point to all kinds of activity as a sign of my dedication. The activity, however, was leading me away from my original goals. Only because I had my ideal written on paper was I able to be objective. I then motivated myself to move toward my original ideal. I still have that essay and refer to it at regular intervals.

Time Frame

Setting a specific *time* for the achievement of a given goal is important because it triggers the subconscious mind to accomplish the goal within that allotted time. Some people will not be motivated unless there is a deadline, and telling themselves that they will accomplish something "as soon as possible" may mean it will never get done.

One year I had a young lady in class who had no problem with a long-range goal. All her life she had wanted to go to Australia and had read everything she could find on the country. She knew a great deal about the people, the terrain, the flowers and the economics of Australia. When I examined her statement of goals, I noticed she had included all of the qualities for effective goal setting except a time frame. She indicated that she wanted to take a three week trip to Australia during their summer but she did not have a date of departure. I suggested she clarify the date. She responded by saying that she really didn't know how long it would take to acquire the necessary resources and time to make such a trip. I told her to take a guess or simply create a date. It was mid-January at that time, so she took that day's date and added one year.

I completely forgot about the incident. One day after school in mid-October I was preparing to leave Cleveland for Columbus to give a lecture at Ohio State University. I gathered the mail from my box, threw it into the car and went on my way. I arrived at the University about a half an hour early and so began opening my mail. To my surprise I found a letter from this woman who had not been in touch with me since the workshop. She was writing to thank me for forcing her to write a goal the previous January. Soon after the class, she had the opportunity to take a part-time job. She immediately thought of the goals she had written down in class, took the job and became so good at it she was offered a full-time position. By September she had acquired not only enough money for a trip to Australia for herself but was able to take her daughter along. Because she wanted to use her time as efficiently as possible, she went to a travel agent to find out what kind of packages were available. The one she found most satisfying was departing on the very day she had written on her paper almost a year before. It is amazing how the subconscious mind works!

Discovering Goals

How often over the years I have heard students tell me, "I believe all of these facts about goal setting, but how do I find out what my goals are?" This is, of course, a very important matter and one that needs careful consideration.

First of all, quiet is the most effective place to clarify goals. By creating inner quiet you can contact your subconscious mind and break through all the barriers of time and space. You can then be very efficient, very effective and very precise about future goals.

A long time ago, I attended a workshop for business executives that was being presented by a capable professor from a prestigious university on the east coast. He suggested to participants that they go into a time of quiet for at least ten or fifteen minutes each morning and each evening. In the morning, he suggested that this quiet time be spent looking over the goals they wanted to achieve that day. At the end of the day they were to review all the goals they had achieved. This practice, he promised, would constantly reinforce the fact that they could set and achieve goals.

He added that it was important to take time off once a month to do exactly the same thing. He suggested that each of the executives get to a quiet place, visit a park or rent a room, where they would not be disturbed for a full day. During that time, he suggested that they look over what had been accomplished in the previous month and look ahead to the following month, being specific about the goals that they wanted to achieve in the major areas of their lives. He concluded by suggesting each person spend at least a weekend every year repeating the same procedure for annual planning.

By the time he finished describing this method of daily, monthly and yearly quiet time for setting and reviewing goals, I was reminded of the same schedule that was written into our lives as friars. From the very first day we entered the Order, we were taught how to meditate for one half hour each morning and evening for exactly the same purpose. We were told in the morning to visualize the things that we wanted to accomplish or the kind of personal characteristics that we wanted to develop and at the end of the day to review our progress. Each month we had a complete day set aside in which the community experienced what was called a Day of Recollection. It was a day of sustained quiet when each of us could look back over the past month and plan the coming month. We were also required, and are still required, to take a full week each year for what is called a personal retreat. During that time, we are to reflect on what has happened over the past year and to look ahead and plan for the coming year.

I was rather curious to find out where the professor had gotten his information since it was so similar to what I had learned in the seminary. At a break, I went to see him and asked him where he got his material. He looked sheepishly from one side to the other and in a low tone of voice told me, "Father, I swiped it from you." He then proceeded to tell me that for years it had been a hobby of his to read the lives of the saints, whom he considered the most successful human beings of history. All of these people followed a similar schedule for planning their spiritual growth. "If it worked for them" he said, "it would work for these business executives."

If it seems impossible for you to create these specific slots of quiet in your life, then create other slots of quiet whenever you can. Our lives in 20th century society are busy and we all have the same problems with time management. In my own life I rise earlier in order to have the quiet time that I need. I also get away from the office every afternoon for physical exercise and quiet time. At the end of each day I meditate before I go to sleep.

When you take the time for quiet is irrelevant; *that* you take time for quiet is essential. Truly, I do not know of any other way human beings can access their inner potential and get a clear view of their future goals.

Goals and God's Will

As I stated earlier, God wants for each of us that which will bring us the highest fulfillment. It makes sense then to discover what that direction is and set your goals accordingly.

Let me share a few examples. A dear friend of mine completed high school and entered pharmacy school simply because friends were moving in that direction. Without paying particular attention to his direction, he worked hard and became a registered pharmacist. After being involved in that work for only a few months, he realized that he really could not be happy there. At this point, he spent a lot of time alone considering his future. He realized that he actually wanted to be a dentist. He went back to school, using his skill as a pharmacist to earn the necessary money and became a dentist. Since that time, he has earned an outstanding name in the field and is very happy and fulfilled in that profession.

More recently, I met a gentleman who shared some intimate aspects of his life with me. As a young man, when all of his friends were getting married, he felt the "normal" thing to do was to follow suit. The night before the wedding, he told his best friend that he didn't want to get married and wished he couldn't. After many years of unhappiness, he began to spend time alone giving serious consideration to himself and his life. He came face to face with the fact that his sexual orientation was homosexual, not heterosexual. He has since gotten divorced and is happier than he has been in years!

In chapter seven of this book, we will spend more time considering intuition and conscience. These are two human faculties that help us get in touch with inner, Divine Presence. By "listening" to that personalized guidance, we can know what goals are best for each of us. By making those goals our own, we can give direction to our lives and find the fulfillment that is our human heritage.

SUGGESTED ACTIVITIES

Life Wheel

1. Each spoke of the life wheel represents one of the major categories for goal setting. You may choose to change or rename categories for yourself, but don't forget the values they balance.

Directions:

a. If the very center of the circle represents 0 and means 'not at all satisfied' and 10 is 'as satisfied as you can imagine being,' put an **X** in each segment indicating your current level of personal satisfaction in that area.

b. Now draw a "circular" line connecting each **X** (moving in a clockwise direction). Shade in the center space.

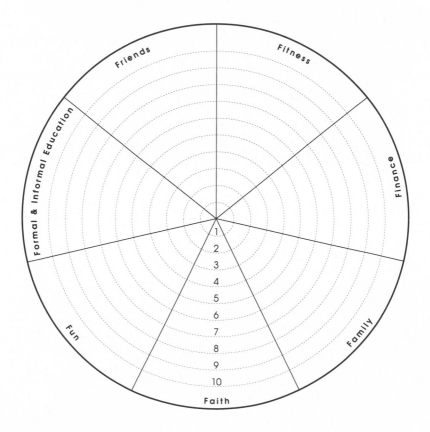

c. What do you notice?
  • Is the picture different than you expected?
  • How do you feel about your picture?
  • Do you see things you want to change?
  • Is the emphasis where you thought it would be?

Note that the title of the diagram is "Life Wheel." If you have created the semblance of a wheel, then more than likely you have balance in your life. However, if you have a "flat tire" you may be finding your life journey a bit bumpy and uncomfortable. You may need balance in the area of goal setting.

2. Write some goals that you are presently working to achieve.

3. Write some goals in areas where you need balance.

4. Check the goals you have written to see if they are specific. Does the challenge excite you? Did you clarify a time frame?

5. Spend a few moments visualizing the accomplishment of the goals you have written down. As each one is accomplished, what effect will it have on the shape of your life wheel?

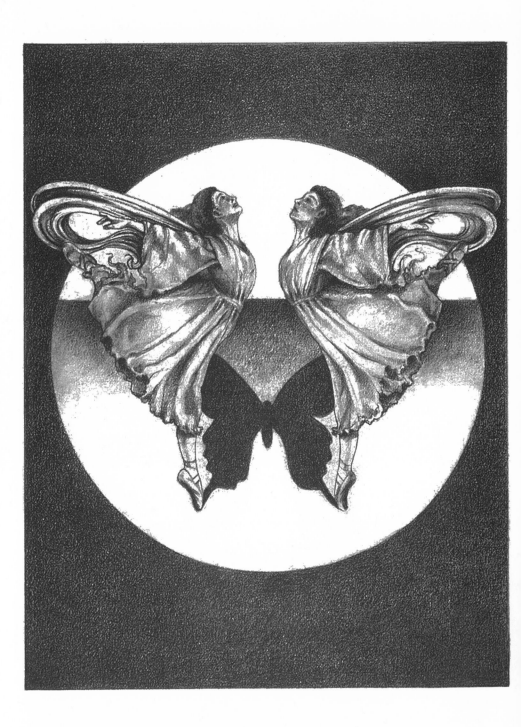

7

ENTHUSIASM, CREATIVITY AND CONSCIENCE

In the past, the spiritual dimension of the human person was the sole responsibility of theology. In Western culture, the spiritual dimension of the human person was relegated exclusively to the church for an extended period of history.

At present, however, health specialists and other professionals are concerning themselves with the spiritual dimension of life. What was laying on of hands has become the study of therapeutic touch. Meditation and contemplation are described in terms of relaxation and visualization. Prayer is described in terms of affirmation. What was known as faith healing is called spontaneous remission and is studied by brain/mind specialists. The reading of minds and hearts is being studied in terms of thought transference. The perception of events in distant places is being studied in terms of remote viewing.

Even the reality of God is being described scientifically in terms of universal intelligence, cosmic energy and unlimited potential. Unfortunately, many people get trapped (by the rather natural, human resistance to change or by attachment to what they think they have already clarified in their life) into seeing what is happening as a threat or crisis, rather than as an expanding opportunity. Because of the vastness of this shift in the direction of scientific study, terms like enthusiasm, creativity, and conscience which have both a theological and a scientific connotation become increasingly important.

Enthusiasm

Etymologically, the word enthusiasm comes from the Greek *en* + *theos*, meaning "in god" or "with god." The dictionary defines it as "inspired or possessed by god." An enthusiastic person, therefore, is one functioning with the unlimited, internal energy that theologically is referred to as "God." Scientifically, an enthusiastic person is one functioning with the same unlimited, internal energy, but it is described in terms of intuitive access to universal intelligence or insight into cosmic energy. Although the descriptions are different, the human experience is the same.

Theologians teach that human beings cannot effectively function without God, and scientists declare that enthusiasm is essential to achieving anything of value. Both proclaim that nothing can be accomplished without their own brand of "it."

Whether you prefer one mode of explanation or the other doesn't really matter. It is the human experience we want to consider here and how we can use this internal and unlimited energy to enrich our lives.

Internal Source
Enthusiasm can be activated from within or it can be stimulated from outside the individual. The former method is most important since control is then in the hands of the person involved and it can be turned on at will.

Review your goals. One way to generate enthusiasm is to have a goal in mind—something that is important to you, something you want with a passion. Once the goal is in place, the desire to achieve it will drive you to overcome obstacles, to live with inconvenience or even pain, and move you to do extraordinary things.

In my life the very thought of 'Franciscan Priest' as my personal goal always excited me. From that day in first grade when the goal became clear to the very day of ordination, I could be motivated to do anything because of my desire for the goal. Sometimes that energy lay quietly inside me and sometimes it externalized itself with a great deal of activity, but it was always there!

It is easy to be or become enthusiastic when you are doing something that has meaning for you. It may be something as simple as waxing a new car or something as challenging as an Olympic gold medal, but if the activity is important to you, enthusiasm will spontaneously well up inside of you.

Sometimes, however, you may be distracted from important goals by pressing responsibilities or unpleasant situations. When that happens, it is necessary to consciously review your goals to generate enthusiasm.

Nancy was 18 when she left home for the first time to attend junior college. After four months, she was involved in semester exams and having a difficult time. She was disgusted with the entire struggle and took a break to visit a friend and classmate. They started to talk about the trip they would soon be taking to be with their families for the holidays. Nancy related how she had wanted to return home with high grades as a way of thanking her parents for the opportunity of attending college. She began to visualize a report card in her hand with the grades she desired. She could see the look on her parents' faces when she handed it to them. With those clear images the girls began to think of the excitement of the trip home, the crowds and the pleasant ride. Before long Nancy was feeling better about herself and her preparation for exams. She left the conversation eager to return to her studies, feeling enthusiastic again about her goals.

You can recall similar circumstances where you were having a difficult time, but the thought of some future event helped you to re-focus so that you could generate enthusiasm for what had to be done. What is important to note is that images of future goals become triggers that turn on the powerful energies of excitement and anticipation. In that way you can at any time you wish generate enthusiasm from inside your own person.

Employ the "act as if" principle. Giving direction to your feelings is another way to generate enthusiasm when you need it. Clearly identifying a goal AND acting as if you have already achieved it, can generate enthusiasm that will carry you toward achievement.

Feelings may seem to be nebulous, but they can be controlled. Having been trained for the entertainment industry early in life, I learned to use the "act as if" principle at a very young age. We were taught that our job was to make people feel good and the way to do that was to feel good yourself.

One evening during a performance, I announced an act and walked offstage where there was supposed to be someone holding my accordion so that I could strap it on and return as part of the backup. However, no one was there so I had to call for assistance which I did quietly but with anger. My back, of course, was to the audience, and when the accordion finally arrived, I first put on a smile, turned around, and walked onto the stage making believe that I was having the time of my life, when in fact I was very upset inside. As I got involved in acting "happy" I began to feel happy, and the anger simply disappeared.

The next time you lose your enthusiasm, try this little technique. Act as if you feel differently and then pay attention to the results. By turning on enthusiasm in this way, you can make your life more exciting and productive.

External Source

Thus far we have been discussing how enthusiasm can be generated from within. It is also possible to generate enthusiasm from outside the self. It is important to note this option because there are times when we all need the assistance of others to pick up our spirits.

Imagine yourself coming home from a long day at work feeling very tired. As you arrive home, you realize that you have made a commitment to attend a party that evening. Although you don't feel like going, you get yourself ready (only to fulfill the commitment). You arrive at the party with some resentment, but as you experience the music, the decorations, people laughing and carrying on, you begin to feel the excitement and before long you get caught up in the spirit and get actively involved in celebrating yourself.

When you begin to feel down, and you have a difficult time picking yourself up, it is a great blessing to have friends and/

or places where you can go to get a boost. Of course it is much better to be able to activate enthusiasm from within yourself but it doesn't hurt to have the second option available as an alternative.

Having close friends who think the way you do, or a support group who understands your problems and ideals is a powerful and sometimes necessary help to keep you balanced and happy. In fact, Napoleon Hill in his book *Think and Grow Rich* said that this kind of group is necessary for anyone who has challenging goals and high ideals. This group becomes a buffer between you and a world that may be negative or in some cases even destructive.

When I was part of a high school music department, one of my support groups was the music staff itself. We thought alike and did what we could to lift the spirits of those around us. Sometimes when we would walk by the general office and see frowning faces, we would walk up to the large glass windows, put our faces directly against the glass, smile and wave until those on the inside began to smile. We then went on our way. We got the reputation of being "strange" but when we did such "strange things" we were able to lift the spirits of others as well as our own!

Creativity

The word creativity comes from the Latin *creare* or "creator" meaning "to bring into being" or "the one who brings something into being." This term is as related to Supreme Being as the word enthusiasm. Creativity points to the act of bringing into being; enthusiasm points to the power behind that act. Both are theologically related to God.

Parapsychology refers to these concepts when dealing with the human mind and human potential. Creativity is considered a property of the mind, by which it is able to produce something that has never before existed. It is an aspect of Universal Intelligence.

Traditionally, study and involvement in the fine arts has been THE way of training human beings to use this creative dimension. Unfortunately, the educational system in the West has relegated fine arts to the fringe. Our educational system essentially has become a left-brain system, putting emphasis on logic, language, math, and deductive skills. As a result, right-brain activities such as intuition, painting, music, dance and psychic skills have taken a backseat.

Creativity Generates Growth

When functioning as a music instructor and chairperson of the music department in an all boys' school, I felt it my duty to develop some balance in right/left brain training. Together with the art department we insisted that every student be required to obtain one full credit of fine arts before graduation. This was the early 1960s when we were still feeling the impact of Sputnik and the government was putting emphasis on science. We encountered a good deal of opposition to our fine arts policy, not only from teachers and administration but also from parents.

In one case, a young man who had a great deal of natural ability in math came to the school with the express purpose of majoring in math. Both he and his parents wanted to substitute math courses for music and art courses. We were adamant about the fine arts requirement and insisted this youngster get background in the arts. To his amazement and pleasure, he found that he had a great deal of creative ability. He began to produce jewelry in art class that was so beautiful and unique that it was often displayed in the art showcase. Many of his pieces were purchased by staff members. When he moved into his junior year, he chose to take an art elective and started developing painting skills. He did go on to major in math, but, at the same time, became aware of and began to use his creative talents in the arts. Today he is a much more balanced human being because of that training.

Experience of the "Creative"
Connects Us with the "Sacred"

I did not always realize the essential similarity between aesthetic and religious experience. As a teenager I had an encounter with the arts that had a profound impact on the rest of my life. One Sunday morning as I was paging through the newspaper on the floor of our living room, I saw a full-page ad for the Sadler Wells Ballet Company from England. They were touring the country and had scheduled a single performance in Omaha. Somehow, on the inside, I knew I had to be there, that it was important. I asked my parents for permission and the money to go to the theater. They suggested I ask around the neighborhood to find someone who might be interested in going with me. No one, of course, knew anything about ballet so I ended up going to the theater alone. I had a seat on the aisle high in the balcony. When the lights dimmed and the orchestra began, I was transported to a completely different level of awareness. The ballet, *Coppelia* by Delibes, a light and humorous ballet in three acts, gave me an experience I shall never forget! When the ballet was finished, I did not want to disturb the wonderful feeling I was experiencing so I sat in my seat, waited for everyone to clear the theater and then very quietly found my way out a side door. I walked through the streets of downtown for a long time, basking in a euphoria that was new to me. While I walked I was aware that this intuitive experience of beauty led me into prayer. I was puzzled by the fact that a humorous ballet could trigger such a deep connection with God.

It wasn't until years later when I was finishing my M.A. in music education at Case-Western Reserve that I came in touch with a doctoral dissertation explaining the essential similarity between the aesthetic and religious experience. It was then that I realized the arts are capable of breaking through the senses to touch the fundamental core of human experience the same way that religious experience breaks through the senses to touch the same reality. Experiencing Beauty is similar to experiencing Divinity.

Creativity—the Language of Feelings

All of the fine arts communicate feeling—an essential part of every human being. By coming in contact with sculpture, music, dance, architecture, etc., we can feel in ways that help us be more sensitive to the human condition. These experiences are an important way for people to grow emotionally.

Beethoven, for example, had to cope with enormous difficulty in his life. Over and over again he was frustrated in love, living a painful and lonely life. Imagine the panic he felt when, at the height of his career, he realized that he was beginning to lose his hearing. At first it was just a slight buzzing in his ears, but as time went on he realized his hearing would eventually disappear altogether.

As he grappled with daily life, he tried to determine whether he should continue to live as a deaf person and give up his music career, or whether he should simply take his life. That struggle went on for nearly ten years!

During that time, Beethoven began to create what we know today as the Fifth Symphony. The four notes at the beginning of the work have been compared to fate knocking on the door. He took that tiny motif and created an entire movement in which he expressed his feelings. When you listen to this music you can begin to feel what Beethoven felt. In the second movement, it is as if Beethoven has reached a little oasis in his desert. This section of the work expresses what he was feeling when he was involved enough in his work to forget about his problem. In the third movement, Beethoven is struggling again. At the end of this segment there is a long, suspenseful passage where the timpani produce a slow roll that goes on for pages and the violins do a tremolo for several moments. The suspense is intense. Then, without a break, the music moves into the fourth movement, glorious and magnificent. After struggling for so long with this personal problem, Beethoven decided he would not give up his music, even though he was going deaf, nor would he take his life. He created a third option—he would live and compose as a deaf musician. The feelings attached to this thought process are profound and can be experienced by the listener.

He continued on, writing some of his most important works and never hearing any of them with his physical ears. How wonderful it is to share intimate and momentous feelings with a master like Beethoven by simply listening to his music.

All of the fine arts communicate in the same way. Gibran's collection of poems under the title of *The Prophet* can open a door to new and varied experience of feeling. Perhaps you can take the time to acquire this volume if you do not already have it and read one or the other of his poems on important subjects like Love, Children, Joy and Sorrow, Friends, Giving, etc.

You too have the ability to express your feelings about life by using your creative talent. You too are poet, painter, musician, sculptor, designer; you are a unique artist capable of producing beauty in your life and in our world. I believe these statements are true. Do you? (Remember the theory: what you put into your mind and brain will materialize in your life. Think positively and you will actualize your creative talent; think negatively and you will suppress that talent!)

Conscience

The word "conscience" is derived from the Latin meaning "with knowledge." In theological terms it is defined as a faculty, power, or principle enjoining good acts. Scientifically it refers to a part of the superego that transmits commands and admonitions to the ego. In other words, conscience implies the reality of an inner reservoir of information, common to all human beings, that can be used for making appropriate decisions in life.

As discussed in chapter two, when human beings are in a meditative state or altered state, it is possible to break through limits of time and space and be in touch with Universal Intelligence. In other words, we have the capability of dipping into the past, present or future for information to solve problems or get direction. We also have the ability to access information anywhere in the universe for this purpose. With that kind of data base, it is clear that all of us are equipped with a mechanism that can help us in all of life's challenges.

When dealing with moral and ethical issues, there are two areas that must be taken into consideration, law and conscience.

Peoples' Needs Come Before the Law

In any group or society, rules and regulations are necessary for the common good. However, there is a norm that states "the law is created for the people, not the people for the law." In other words, the law exists solely to improve the quality of life for the people.

Traffic laws, for example, are created for the safety of all the people. However, exceptions are made in the law to accommodate the needs of the people. When a funeral entourage moves through the city, there is often a representative of the law present to allow the procession to move through red lights—this is a consideration made by the law to take care of a specific need of the people.

Law is General; Conscience is Specific

By its nature, law points in a general direction. The law: "Do good, avoid evil" has been accepted for thousands of years all over the planet by every culture but it is a general statement.

Conscience on the other hand is always specific, having to deal with particular situations in the present. Suppose a child living on the streets of New York is in need of food and is without money. The law states: "Thou shalt not steal," but the child still needs food. The child picks up an apple from a fruit stand and runs. The child realizes that stealing is wrong, but in this specific case makes a decision that it is more important to survive than to obey the law.

The law simply cannot be stated so as to include every particular situation. For that very reason we have an intricate and complex system to apply the law in specific cases.

On the other hand, all human beings live in the now and have to make decisions daily. One eye, as it were, is focused on the law, the other on particular needs and circumstances.

Law is Fallible; Conscience is Infallible

Generally law is written and static while life is in constant motion. As a result, written law becomes outdated and must constantly be updated as life circumstances change. This means that there is a large margin for error in law.

On the other hand, conscience is always right. When anyone is in a situation where a decision must be made, they can only make that decision based on the background available and the intuitive sense that is part of the human mechanism. The decision must be made, and at that point conscience will always lead the individual to what is best.

I recently saw a dramatization of a rescue that took place at Niagara Falls. Two young women were in a boat at night, headed for the falls and didn't know it. When they realized what the situation was they tried to move in the opposite direction but could not. They both put on life vests and dove into the water hoping to reach the shore. One girl got close enough to the shore to grab a rope that was thrown to her by a member of the rescue team. The other was too weak to fight the current, so a member of the rescue team tied a rope around himself and dove into the water. He was able to reach the other girl and bring her to safety.

The rules and/or laws to which the rescue team were bound did not demand that they risk their lives, but in this case the young man involved did what he thought was appropriate. It was not something written into the law; but a decision had to be made at that moment and for him it was the correct decision.

Law is Subservient; Conscience is Supreme

The relationship between law and conscience is very clear: conscience must be followed at all costs, even if it means violating the law. No one, for any reason, may ever act contrary to the dictates of conscience.

Theologically, the reason for this statement is the fact that God is with the person making the decision and God would never lead anyone in the wrong direction. Scientifically, the reason is that the person has contact with unlimited knowledge and therefore can know what is best in a particular situation.

Even the Catholic Church, in the document from Vatican II titled, *"Declaration on Religious Liberty,"* dated December 1965, stated: "It is through his conscience that man sees and recognizes the demands of divine law. He is bound to follow this conscience faithfully in all his activity so that he may come to God, who is the last end. Therefore he must not be forced to act contrary to his conscience, nor must he be prevented from acting according to his conscience...."

Francis of Assisi in his Rule of 1223 also stated the supremacy of conscience when he wrote: "Let the friars be obedient to their superiors in everything except what may be contrary to this Rule and their conscience."

In the New Testament St. Paul identified the reality of conscience—a concept that existed in the Old Testament under the title "heart."

Forming Conscience

It is true that everyone has a sense for what is right and wrong but they surely do not always make the same decisions. One of the reasons for this discrepancy is the fact that training, teaching, culture, and religion. all have a part to play in the way a person's conscience is shaped.

It is true that we have an obligation to get as much information as we can before we make an important decision. The fact of the matter is that we are all limited in our human condition and will experience that limit even if we have spent a great deal of time gathering information.

In the end, when the decision must be made, we are obliged to function with the information at hand (limited as it may be). As long as we have made the effort to do our best, God will take care of the rest and "inform" us from within, with the added information needed to make decisions that are appropriate for us and in consideration of those around us.

Application

In the last analysis, when dealing with specific situations in life we must pick up the responsibility of decision making. This important human faculty is what gives us freedom to shape our lives and to create meaning for ourselves. It is not always pleasant to accept this responsibility but it is comforting to know that we have a voice in the way our lives move and shape themselves.

There are a great many unclear and controversial issues in the world and in our lives today: birth control, morality of war, capital punishment, abortion, etc. The comforting part of the reality however is that none of us have to solve these problems for others—in fact, many of them will not be solved, at least not now. However, we have the tools to make our own decisions and to live our own convictions without having to push anyone else anywhere.

Follow your conscience—trust it. Allow others to follow theirs. Accept responsibility for the consequences of your own choices. Help others accept responsibility for the consequences of the decisions they make. This is what it means to be accountable.

Summary

Enthusiasm, creativity and conscience demonstrate the reality that God is present with everyone, all the time, and that we all have a potential that is virtually unlimited.

It is important to note that we will more likely access "the unlimited" in our persons when we function from the meditative state—relaxing and allowing the sub-conscious mind to communicate with us.

Limit and error are aspects of reality as perceived by the conscious mind. Functioning in what is referred to as "the normal waking state" is where we all experience limit and error. It makes sense, therefore, to become skilled in using the "inner mind," "altered consciousness," or "the meditative dimension" where enthusiasm, creativity and conscience reside. Functioning from this dimension can only lead to effective use of the Life Mechanism and bring into your life love, joy, peace, health, happiness and every other good thing!

SUGGESTED ACTIVITIES

1. Think of a time in your life when you were enthusiastic about doing something or achieving something. Consider how you thought about the goal or activity. Review the kinds of activities in which you were involved.

   Now ask yourself what you want to do or accomplish in the future. Think of something you really want. (You may choose something you can't imagine explaining to anyone else, or decide to address a problem area.) What do you have to do to achieve the goal? Let your intuition help you determine what you need. Are you beginning to feel enthusiasm?

2. Think of someone you know who is enthusiastic and make some time to spend with that person.

3. List some of the creative things you have done in the past. Write a poem, paint a picture, create a dance or model some clay (anything creative) to express how you feel right now.

4. Spend some time with a favorite song. How do you feel when you hear this composition? Do you feel the same or differently when you hum the tune? How would your experience differ if the person of your choice were to serenade you with the song? Express your experience in a creative way.

5. Spend 10 or 15 minutes in quiet, either listening to music, taking a walk or just sitting quietly in a comfortable chair. Pay attention to the sounds, the odors, and the images of the situation; reflect on how you feel; simply be.

   At the end of the exercise, pay attention to what you are feeling or how you are feeling. Does the experience give you a sense of contact with the intangible? Do you understand peace a little more? What words can you use to describe the exercise?

CONCLUSION

The Life Mechanism as presented in this volume is meant specifically for you. By understanding that your life is the result of the choices you make, you can understand also that you are the person in charge of the mechanism.

Just because you understand, however, does not mean that you will be successful. After understanding must come action! For many people, this step can be a real challenge. For that reason I would like to suggest here a few things that can get you started.

Change Your Thoughts

First of all, changing your thoughts about yourself and your world is absolutely necessary if you want to experience change in your life. The most effective way of making that change is in meditation. By taking time every day (especially morning and evening) to visualize yourself the way you want to be and to see your world as you would want it to be, you will be feeding your Life Mechanism with the thoughts that will eventually become your reality.

Suppose you want to be a more joyful person. By visualizing yourself doing and saying things that come from a joyful person, you will give your brain the program it needs to create that reality.

Remember too, that your speech is nothing more than a reflection of your thoughts. Therefore, make it a point to talk about the things you want in your life not the things you don't want. If you want health, talk about those things that will produce health. If you want more money, discuss ways and means at your disposal to increase your income. If you want to have more fun, ask others what their resources are and make plans to get involved yourself.

Befriend Like-Minded People

It is essential that you have the support of other human beings if you hope to succeed in your idealism. Having friends who think the way you do becomes a buffer against the negativity of the outside world.

If you already have like-minded friends, make sure you spend time with them regularly (even if that be only by phone or letter). If you do not already have such friends, write a goal to that effect and begin searching. Anyone who has read this book or others like it, and who believes in the process will be able to give you the support you need. High ideals and strong motivation can be sustained for long periods of time only with the support of others. When you are with special friends like these, talk about your successes and share your future plans. When you bump into obstacles, contact them and ask for assistance in seeking solutions. Sharing problems alone is a negative approach; looking for solutions is a positive one.

Weekly or Monthly Meetings

Some of you may be looking for a more structured approach in a formal support group. Here is an outline for a weekly or monthly group meeting.

One hour meetings are most effective. When the leadership is well prepared to lead, a great deal can be accomplished in a short time. We suggest that you indicate the time to begin *and* the time to end. Discipline is an important part of the Life Mechanism and therefore should be reflected in the meeting. Monthly meetings, especially if the group is larger than ten members, can extend to one hour and a half if necessary. However, weekly meetings are ideal. In this case, effective meetings can be accomplished in less than an hour.

When meetings are weekly, we suggest there be a "committee" of four or five people who are willing to share the leadership. With this kind of arrangement, each person can be responsible for one meeting a month and the fifth person can be used as an emergency substitute.

It is best to have the meeting in a neutral place like a community room, a school or church instead of a private home. In this kind of space there is less danger of the meeting becoming a purely social gathering.

Food and/or beverage need not be required; they can get in the way. However "tea and crumpets" after the meeting can allow for more personalized kinds of sharing.

As for the meeting itself, here is a suggested format:
1. Have the group sit in a circle.
2. Begin with one or two minutes of quiet (perhaps with music background) and ask each individual during that time to recall successes (or blessings) they have experienced since the last meeting.
3. The leader then shares a personal success story—a short range goal already achieved or movement toward a long-range goal, a positive experience at home or work, etc. The leader then invites the person on the right or left to continue around the circle. (Individuals who do not want to share may simply say, "I pass.")
4. If the group is studying a book:
   a. Have each person read one chapter before the meeting.
   b. Suggest that everyone, as they read in advance, mark passages in the book with which they strongly agree or disagree. Questions can be written in the margins.
   c. Ask for practical applications of the material.

d. Personal sharing, especially in terms of application, is always valuable. Sometimes the discussion may move away from the subject matter of the book and into something important to the individual or the group. Allow for this kind of eventuality.

e. Do not allow anyone to dominate the group or to use the meeting to bring up one personal problem after another. Discussing problems is negative—discussing solutions is positive.

5. Allow time for announcements about lectures in the area, TV presentations, books, movies, workshops, etc.
6. Close with a group meditation (either recorded or guided by one of the group).
7. In our "energy circles" no one is allowed to leave until they have shared at least three hugs!!!

Final Thoughts

You were meant to have a wonderful time living on this planet. You have a right to family, friends, health, happiness, all the material things you need, love, joy, peace and every other good thing.

Please take at least one thought from this book and put it into practice in your daily life. In that way you can make your life better and hopefully make it still better in the future.

Remember always, it's your life. You owe it to yourself to

LIVE IT UP!!!

REFERENCE MATERIALS

Books

Adair, Margo—*Working Inside Out*
Campbell, Joseph—*The Hero with a Thousand Faces*
Clarke, Jean Illsley—*Self Esteem: A Family Affair*
Dossey, Larry, M.D.—*Recovering the Soul*
Elgin, Duane—*Voluntary Simplicity*
Fox, Matthew—*Coming of the Cosmic Christ*
Harman, Willis—*Global Mind Change*
Harman, Willis and John Hormann—*Creative Work*
Hay, Louise L.—*You Can Heal Your Life*
Houston, Jean—*Possible Human*
Jampolsky, Gerald G., M.D.—*Love is Letting Go of Fear*
LePage, Andy—*Transforming Education*
McWilliams, John-Roger and Peter—*You Can't Afford the Luxury of a Negative Thought*
Ostrander and Schroeder—*Superlearning*
Pearsall, Paul, Ph.D.—*Super Immunity*
Siegel, Bernie, M.D.—*Love, Medicine and Miracles*
Silva, Jose—*Silva Mind Control Method*
Simonton, O. Carl and Stephanie Simonton—*Getting Well Again*
Theobald, Robert—*Rapids of Change*
von Oech, Roger—*A Kick in the Seat of the Pants*

Seminars on Cassettes

Transforming Your Relationship with Money and Achieving Financial Independence, by Joe Dominguez. Six tapes and a workbook.
Success:Full Living, by Fr. Justin Belitz. Five hours of dynamic presentation of the material in this book.

Most of these resources may be obtained from
Knowledge Systems Inc.
7777 West Morris St.
Indianapolis, IN 46231
phone: 317-241-0749 fax: 317-248-1503

Cassette Tapes

Basic Relaxation, by Therese Ann Coddington A tape specifically designed for people who are beginning meditation or who are having trouble relaxing.

A Universal Morning and Evening Meditation, by Fr. Justin Belitz, O.F.M. A set of two meditations, one for morning and one for evening. The image of light is used to represent God. It is created for people of any faith.

Positive Self-Image, by Fr. Justin Belitz, O.F.M., and Therese Ann Coddington. The purpose of this tape is to help the meditator improve self-image. One side explains the process of how mind and brain create self-image. The other side is a meditation based on positive affirmations designed to improve anyone's self-image.

Music for Meditation, by Flutist: Sr. Barbara Piller, O.S.F., and Harpist: Mary Catherine Wild. A tape of music appropriate for meditation. Side 1 is flute only, and Side 2 is harp only.

The above cassette tapes may be obtained from The Franciscan Hermitage or Knowledge Systems, Inc.

Magazines

Brain / Mind Bulletin—P.O. Box 44221, Los Angeles, CA 90042
Creation—Bear & Co., Inc., Santa Fe, NM 87504-2860
Daily Word—Unity Village, MO 64065
Guidebook for the '90s—7777 W. Morris St., Indianapolis, IN 46231
Noetic Sciences Review—475 Gate Five Rd., Suite 300, Sausalito, CA 94699

Workshop

SUCCESS:FULL LIVING is available in the form of a workshop by Fr. Justin Belitz. Half-day, full day or two-day formats can be arranged. For details and bookings contact The Hermitage at the address on the following page.

THE FRANCISCAN HERMITAGE

The Hermitage is a healing center dedicated to the spiritual emotional, physical, intellectual and professional growth and formation of persons of all persuasions and circumstances.

Located in Indianapolis on seven acres of wooded grounds overlooking Fall Creek, The Hermitage serves as a retreat center for all those concerned with their personal or spiritual journey. It offers both the space and means to explore many avenues of growth by sponsoring a variety of workshops, lectures, nationally know speakers and ongoing support groups. Programs of The Hermitage are currently available across the United States and throughout Australia.

The Hermitage was founded in 1984 in the belief that at times all of us need assistance in discovering and pursuing knowledge of our uniqueness and of our deeper selves. Participating in programs of The Hermitage expands awareness of oneself as both teacher and learner. It provides an atmosphere of freedom for people to get in touch with the divine dimension of their humanity and tap into it for the creativity necessary to serve our times.

HERMITAGE

3650 East 46th Street
Indianapolis, In 46205
phone: 317-545-0742